STUART,

ALL THE BEST
FOR NEXT HALF-
CENTURY!

MATS

(SVEN-GORAN COUNTRY)

GLORIOUS VASA

Fact checking: Erland Sellberg Translation: Kim Loughran
Design: Patric Leo
Color separation, printing and binding: Fälth & Hässler, Värnamo, Sweden, 1999
Printed on Munken Lynx 150 gsm.

ISBN 91-89204-17-4

GLORIOUS VASA

The Magnificent Ship & 17th Century Sweden

TEXT ERLING MATZ PHOTOGRAPHS HANS HAMMARSKIÖLD

Contents

SVPER SATIS EST

A TIME OF LIONS

The lion symbolises not only strength, action, power and courage, but also nobility. The lion spares defenceless enemies. King Gustavus Adolphus was known as the Lion of the North. Did he live up to his image?

A Saxon cavalry standard. Among spoils from the Thirty Years War.

Lions for Fun, Lions for Fright

LIONS ROARING, lions playing, noble lions, pugnacious lions, lions at rest, lions on their feet and lions running. When the royal ship Vasa set sail on the 10th of August, 1628, she was decorated with 500 sculptures, with the lion as the dominating motif. A total of 60 lions clamber over the mighty vessel. All are handsome, muscular males with wild and voluminous manes. The prime specimen is the figurehead lion. Roaring, it leaps forward. Its mane is of glittering gold, its mouth blood-red and its tail stretched aggressively flat. The most remarkable lion is the one on the ship's rudder. With its tail between its legs, it clings to the vertical stern.

The lion sculptures are realistic, even though Swedes had extremely limited knowledge of the African beasts four hundred years ago. King Erik XIV tried to acquire a lion for his coronation ceremony in 1561. This would amuse the guests and bolster royal power and glory. But the attempt failed. No continental principality was willing to give up such a spectacular animal to send as a gift to an insignificant little nation somewhere in the north. The coronation was held with no royal lion in attendance. Several decades later, Erik's brother Johan was given a lion as a gift from England. Another lion came to Sweden in 1648, as part of the treasure the Swedes brought home from a sacked Prague. The booty included arms, silver and gold, jewellery and precious stones, artworks by Michelangelo, Rubens and Raphael, magnificent bronze statues, strange scientific instruments, a glove fashioned from human skin and … a live lion.

Sculpted lions adorn the hatches of the Vasa's gunports. There are 48 lions in all, each with a different character. The tar-drenched rope opened or closed the hatch.

Private zoos have existed since antiquity. Owning a beautiful, wild lion, a statuesque horned buffalo, a quaint monkey or a dancing bear spread lustre over the owner. This ancient tradition suited the interest of Swedes in those days when the country was one of the Great Powers in the unusual, the odd and the magnificent.

The Prague lion was caged in the newly built Lion Den at the Stockholm royal palace, known as the Three Crowns. The court put on animal baiting performances that were considered distressing by contemporary public opinion – and this was during a time when public whippings and executions were the norm. A clergyman called Jonas Petri visited the Lion Den and summarised the depressing spectacle: "A lion and a buffalo were first let in. When the lion stood up, the buffalo charged its chest, almost turning the lion over. Upon that, the lion's interest in the buffalo ended."

But why did a ship, built in the cold, distant North, carry such an unusual pride? Firstly, these animals shared only their appearance with the real lion, *Pantera*

A noble lion will not take offence at a little dog licking its ear. The painted replica of a sculpture from the Vasa tells us that a lion will spare a weak opponent.

The lion was used as a symbol in a variety of ways. This king of the jungle measures time, opening his mouth and moving his eyes at the hour. The lion timepiece was brought to Sweden during the Thirty Years' War.

leo. The African lion is a sluggish, tranquil beast. And the hunter and sprinter is the female, not the maned male. Nor is her hunting skill impressive; only one chase of ten ends in success.

But symbolic lions have far more radiance than real wild lions and the moth-eaten ones of private zoos. According to legend, lions and eagles can look directly at the sun, absorbing from it their divinely gifted power. Thus, lions have for thousands of years symbolised heavenly force, the power of princes, strength and courage.

And also nobility. In legend, the lion spares defenceless foes. This explains why a lion with a silly grin is portrayed stepping over a wounded soldier on a Saxon cavalry standard captured by the Swedes during the Thirty Years' War. It also explains why a little dog and a lion are playing with each other on the Vasa's bow. The lion is here the protector of the weak and defenceless. More often, the lion symbolises power and strength. Statues of lions stood guard outside the royal palaces of Mesopotamia and Babylon. King Solomon decorated his throne with likenesses of lions and the invincible Samson killed a lion in a duel. The abhorrent Emperor Nero loved spectacles and hitched lions to his chariot whenever he

At the top of the Vasa's stern, two griffins crown a young king. Underneath are the letters GARS *– Gustavus Adolphus Rex Sueciae, Gustavus Adolphus King of Sweden. The full Swedish coat of arms is under the coronation scene.*

The Vasa's figurehead is three-and-a-half metres long and weighs approximately half a tonne. Originally it was painted, with gilded details.

Three hundred years ago, the Swedish King was given a lion by the court of Lisbon. Its lair was at the "Lion Field" in Stockholms' Djurgården Park. Sweden's oldest preserved lion is now to be found at Gripsholm Palace.

Lions formed the feet of Queen Maria Eleonora's tin coffin. Maria Eleonora, the wife of Gustavus Adolphus, died in 1655.

appeared before the Roman people. The Vikings, too, used the lion symbolically. A carved lion's head was found on the old Norse Oseberg Ship, which dates from the 9th century. In the 13th century, lions were appearing on royal and noble heraldry.

The magnificent Swedish coat of arms, high up on the Vasa's stern, is also from the Middle Ages. Two lions rampant, their hind legs muscular, their jaws open in wild roar and their manes erect. They are grasping the royal coat of arms in their paws. In that century, it showed the sheaf of grain of the Vasa dynasty. But the coat of arms has a longer history. As early as 1275, King Magnus 'The Barn-Lock' made the royal lion his own and the Swedish people's emblem.

In the early 1600s, there was a lion legend abroad in Europe. A lion from the Kingdom of the Night would fight and defeat the black eagle. It is a prophecy from the Book of Revelations, with another reference in the vision of the learned Swiss physician and mystic, Philippus Paracelsus. In the mid-1500s, Paracelsus had a vision in which he saw a young king, a lion of the North, triumph over the mightiest dynasty in Europe – the German eagle, the Hapsburgian emperor.

Lions have decorated the coats of arms of noble Swedes since the 13th century. The animal is often on its hind legs and in left profile.

The tale was spread in Sweden by one of King Gustavus Adolphus's teachers, the mystic Johannes Bureus. He wrote:

A Northland lion
On third watch stays
And is at guard
As the Good Book says.

The leonine mantle suited the Swedish King just as it had Hercules, the Greek hero. The King had read Paracelsus, and it can be deduced that the multitude of lions on the Vasa were symbolising the King himself, his power and his mission. This applies especially to the proud figurehead lion: as it leaps in ferocious attack, it is protecting its heart with a shield. The shield shows a sheaf of grain, Swedish vase, and a crown. This was the coat of arms of Gustav Adolf and the dynasty of the Vasa family. Which gave the ship its name.

"We await the Swedish King as the Jews await the Messiah," in the words of the German field marshal, Wallenstein. In 1630, the Lion of the North leapt.

The Lion of the North

A FATHER WHO REFUSED to genuflect before his king at a coronation. A mother so frugal she once asked her guests to eat the bones of the fish they had been served. And a comet to indicate that a great prince was about to be born. Gustavus Adolphus had a remarkable heritage. He was born at the royal palace, the Three Crowns, between seven and eight o'clock on the morning of 9 December, 1594. His mother ordered a distinctly unprincely cot: according to preserved records, it cost one *daler*, as much as a jug and a half of wine.

That little Gustavus Adolphus's birthplace was the royal palace did not signify that he was destined to be king. When he was born, his cousin Sigismund had recently been crowned, and there was little to indicate that Gustavus Adolphus would one day ascend the Swedish throne. The only sign was the great ambition of the infant's father, Duke Karl, he who refused to go down on one knee at the crowning of the Polish Sigismund on 19 February, 1594. The duke's wife, Kristina, observed the scene. At around that time, she became pregnant. Gustavus Adolphus was born nine months later.

The allegorical painting of King Gustavus Adolphus in Roman armour was painted after the King's death by David Klöcker Ehrenstrahl. The sculpture in the foreground, showing a warrior in Roman armour, had a prominent position on the Vasa.

It shortly became apparent, however, that the child would one day assume the throne: when Gustavus Adolphus was three, his father led a revolt against King Sigismund. After a couple of years of fighting, the Riksdag, or parliament, in Stockholm deposed Sigismund. But the struggle for monarchical power would affect Gustavus Adolphus throughout his life. Sigismund could never reconcile the loss of Sweden and skirmishes between the two cousins were not to cease until they both died. As if it were planned, both died in 1632. Gustavus Adolphus was killed in battle at Lützen on 6 November. Sigismund had died of aches and age a half-year before.

From an early age, Gustavus Adolphus was known to his contemporaries for his stubbornness and courage, frugality and perseverance. Anecdotes about him abound. When he was only about one year old, Gustavus Adolphus was playing in a field. Duke Karl muttered a warning about snakes. "Give me a stick and I'll kill them," replied the tot, who had only recently learnt to walk and talk. "Do not believe he is afraid," noted the proud father.

Gustavus Adolphus was impulsive throughout his life. His closest adviser, Chancellor Axel Oxenstierna, later talked about the King's "hot-headedness," both in government affairs and in battle.

Celestial phenomena and strange occurrences dogged Gustavus Adolphus. The German astronomer Schmidt discovered strange outbursts in the Leo constella-

Poland's King Sigismund never gave up hope of regaining the throne of Sweden. Swedish war propaganda portrayed the Poles as untrustworthy and cowardly. A sculpture on the Vasa shows a Pole hiding under a table like a dog.

tion; a tanner called Kotter had a vision of the Tree of Life shaken while lions fought; dumb people learned to speak and a woman gave birth to a son the size of a three-year-old, dressed at birth in boots, helmet and armour, and carrying a kitbag.

But the mystical metamorphosis from foetus to warrior in the womb is only slightly stranger than Sweden's swift transformation in the first decades of the 17th century. From a mediaeval, poverty-ridden, agrarian country was born a thoroughly organised military state. Behind this structure stood Gustavus Adolphus himself and his closest men. For centuries since, academics and others have debated their motive force. One reason was certainly the not-uncommon desire rulers have to make their kingdoms richer, greater and more powerful.

Another reason was the threat from Sigismund in Poland and a third the threat from the powerful Emperor Ferdinand II of Hapsburg and his allies in the Catholic League.

The threat from Ferdinand became acute when the emperor tried to expand his sphere northwards at the end of the 1620s. In 1628, he appointed his chief of staff Wallenstein "General of the Oceanic and Baltic Seas" and laid siege to the important port of Stralsund on the Baltic coast. It was more than a provocation; it was a direct threat to Sweden and its interests. As the King declared in the winter of 1627: "As one wave follows another, the Popish league approaches us."

The King wanted to avoid a war within Sweden's borders at any cost. As a teenager, he had seen the effect of an army moving across countryside. At that time, he fought in the bloody border battles with Denmark. The Swedish provinces of Småland and Öland and the Danish province of Blekinge were ravaged by both Swedish and Danish troops and the 16-year-old learned the vicious rules of combat: pillage, burn and slaughter.

In a letter, he described with some pride how he had burnt down 24 parishes and reduced the town of Vä to ashes. They had, he wrote, "ran rampant, pillaged, burned and killed as we pleased." The King led an attack himself on Kristianopel, a little Danish border town. According to one story, he disguised himself and his soldiers as Danish troops and tricked his way into the town. When they left, all that remained of Kristianopel was a smoking heap of ashes. Men, women and children had all perished. According to Danish accounts, many were put to death while still asleep in their beds, and hatred of Swedes persisted for several generations. Kristianopel became one of the main strongholds of the pro-Danish partisans when Blekinge province became Swedish in 1658.

Lit beacons meant that the enemy was close by. Beacon fires often burned along the coast of the southern province, Småland, in the 1610s. (next pages)

"Nowhere are we weaker than within our borders," believed the King. Which made attack the best defence. The Estate of Peasantry in the Swedish *Riksdag* or parliament agreed and offered to recruit young men to the army as long as there would be no ravaging of Swedish farmlands. "It is far better we tether our horses in the enemy's yard than he tethers his in ours," goes a famous quote from the Peasantry at the time. They agreed to an attack against the emperor as long as the battles were fought on German soil and not Swedish. Nonetheless, Swedes were still weary from all the long wars, against Denmark, Russia and Poland, fought by Gustavus Adolphus's father and bequeathed to him. There were protests and riots across the country against conscription and taxes. In 1624, there was a mutiny among soldiers in a town in Småland province. Many of them were executed. In 1627, a tailor called Mattias in the town of Orsa led the entire town in rebellion

and was executed for his trouble. The list could most certainly be made longer.

And the religious motive? Was not Sweden forced into involvement in the Thirty Years' War by the Catholic threat? The King was one of those who declared this to be the reason. The pure Lutheran faith had to be defended against the Catholic counter-reformation. This easy explanation was spread by Lutheran clergy in Sweden and northern Germany. It was a noble reason for fighting that no one could or dared question. Three people were executed in Stockholm in 1624, accused of harbouring sympathy for the Catholic cause.

But reality is seldom so simple, so black-or-white. In fact, several of Sweden's allies were Catholics. For many years, Sweden had a pact with Catholic France, where Cardinal Richelieu was the leading politician.

Another, less noble, motive was alleged by a French lawyer, Charles Ogier. He spent some time in Sweden in 1634 and wrote about the country and its inhabitants in a remarkably sober and insightful diary. "It is thus with Swedes," wrote Ogier, "that they believe other peoples look down upon them and despise them, since these others have a surplus of what Swedes most value. And Swedes believe that foreigners scorned them for their poverty and shortcomings."

In modern usage: they had an inferiority complex. An inferiority complex towards rich Poland whose King Sigismund proclaimed himself Sweden's rightful

Gustavus Adolphus in wax. The little casket came with a chest of wonders given to the King by the town of Augsburg in 1632. The King is holding a small telescope – an important aid, since he was near-sighted.

The gaming piece, carrying a relief portrait of King Sigismund of Poland, is from a board game. Sigismund and Gustavus were cousins and rivals for the Swedish crown.

The King fell to his knees upon landing on the German island of Usedom on 26 June 1630, a hundred years to the day after the Augsburg Confession. Sweden was intervening in Europe's great war between religions. But there were economic and political reasons in addition to the purely religious. The painting is by Johan Hammer and is from the 1670s.

Correspondence between the King, Axel Oxenstierna and the Council of the Realm was intensive. The spectacles and gloves were given to the King in 1632.

ruler. An inferiority complex towards the rest of Europe, where princes were more powerful, nobles richer and culture and science more adequate. The King's motives were therefore far from unequivocal. They included power, religion, glory, practical politics and a desire to defend and disseminate the Lutheran creed.

Gustavus Adolphus spent a large part of his adult life on military campaigns. Did the warrior king enjoy waging war? Scarcely. "War is neither a stream nor a lake," he wrote, "but a sea of all that is evil." And the King's outburst against his German allies following their rape of Nuremberg is a magnificent display of argument and passion for justice: "You rob and plunder indiscriminately!" roared the King. "As the Lord my God is my witness, my heart feels like bile in my breast when I regard you! I would rather ride naked than be dressed at your cost. And should you wish to rebel, so be it; then my Swedes and my Finns and I would first have a spat with you, so that pieces of us should fly in the air!" He made good speeches, as his daughter, Queen Kristina, would recall in her memoirs.

The first time Gustavus Adolphus saw battle, he was a teenager. It was on difficult terrain at the border between the southern Swedish province of Småland and what was then the Danish province of Blekinge. The Swedish force "ran rampant, pillaged, burned and killed as we pleased," wrote the King.

He most probably preferred army bivouacking to life at home in the capital. In a field army, he was the commander-in-chief but preferably also captain, junior officer, artillery officer and soldier in the ranks – in a word, everything. He was good at improvising and in one letter noted with joviality that he was forced to be both secretary and recorder since his closest aides were lying, injured, in the field hospital: "And I will shortly be forced to become my own batman as well."

Can a Christian king launch an offensive war "untainted by sin," he once asked his teacher, Johannes Bureus. The King struggled to find an answer. At the same time, he was galvanised by proximity to danger. Otherwise, how could he have leapt into a boat and made himself a target during the tumultuous battle on the River Vistula in Poland in 1627 and be hit in the groin by a bullet? How could he have ridden to the crest of a hill in Dirschau in the same year, taunting Polish snipers? A musket ball lodged just above his breastbone. Doctors were unable to remove the ball but the King survived. "Leave it be," he said, "in memory of a life not spent in idleness and cringing." Once, when wishing to impress the Danish king, Gustavus Adolphus let him finger the protuberance made by the bullet.

He was thus unafraid of danger, but of idleness and cringing. The fatal Battle of Lützen can be seen as inevitable. The combination of lack of fear, hot-headedness and near-sightedness – the King saw distant things very dimly – was extremely unfortunate. At Lützen, Gustavus Adolphus lost his bearings and rode his horse right into a group of enemy cavalrymen and was toppled by five German pistol shots and two German sword thrusts.

A Pretty Girl Plays Hell with Your Heart

MY FATHER LOVED women too much, wrote Queen Kristina of King Gustavus Adolphus. And if truth be told, the wilful field commander had a weakness for the ladies and often fell for strong women. Gustavus Adolphus's first and greatest love was Ebba Brahe. Their love story is a touching example of teenage rapture, with all the complications of a folk tale but without the happy ending. The young couple met, fell head over heels in love, and exchanged breathless letters, addressed to "my heart's dearest one".

He was 17 and on his way to war, but swore eternal fidelity and enclosed a forget-me-not in a letter to his love. She had just turned 15 and was a lady-in-waiting in the service of the fairy-tale wicked mistress – in this case, the King's

King Gustavus Adolphus sent flowers to Ebba Brahe. She was fifteen and he seventeen. But their love displeased his mother. One of the King's letters enclosed a pressed forget-me-not.

A miniature of Ebba Brahe is hidden in a little casket of turned ivory.

mother, who makes her life a misery. The King's mother had her own plans for her son. Gustavus Adolphus's determined mother, the dowager Queen Kristina, was the victor. Ebba Brahe was married off to the war hero Jakob De la Gardie. The King's farewell gift to his beloved was a clasp set with diamonds and a letter to her finished with his promise to be, until his death, "your faithful and dutiful friend." And, like a noble lion, he conferred on De la Gardie the title of count only weeks after his marriage proposal. When Ebba and Jakob wed on Midsummer's Day, 1618, the guests comprised everybody of importance in the kingdom, including the hard-hearted widow queen – everyone except the jilted suitor. He had gone to sea to test a new warship. On a wall at Skokloster, the best preserved castle from the Great Power days, someone has scrawled: "A beautiful girl is hell for your soul and purgatory for your wallet." It is a motto that might have been written by the King. In 1616, he was given a son by Margareta Slots. Unfortunately, she already had a husband in Finland. The court chaplain Johannes Rudbeckius did not hesitate to tongue-lash his king: if a common soldier had committed such an offence, he would have paid with his life, but since it is the King who has trespassed, few questions will be asked. Law and order are a spiderweb where small flies are caught but which horseflies break through.

Ebba Brahe's garden pavilion has been preserved, south of Fagersta in south-central Sweden.

The illegitimate son of Gustavus Adolphus and Margareta Slots was given a noble title, Gustav Gustavsson of Vasaborg. He was permitted to use the emblem of the Vasa dynasty, a sheaf of grain, on his coat of arms but a diagonal red band – the bastard string – indicates illegitimacy.

It must be said that the King attempted to do the right thing. The litigious Margareta Slots was given a farm in Uppland province as a royal donation and their son was given a title, Gustav Gustavsson of Vasaborg. His escutcheon is still to be seen in the House of Nobility in Stockholm, displaying a single ribbon – the 'bastard string' – over the coat of arms of the Vasas.

In 1619, three years after his adventure with Margareta Slots, the King was scouring northern Germany for a queen. Again, strong women were pulling the strings and almost sabotaged the entire quest. The lustful king spied Maria Eleonora av Brandenburg. She was a good political match, she was young and she was beautiful. Without having proposed or even having been introduced, the King started preparations for a wedding. The royal castle was decorated, wine was ordered and the nobility was ordered to dress in their finery and hasten to the capital. The King sailed off to fetch his bride, but had to turn back at Kalmar, in southern Sweden. Maria Eleonora's mother, Anna, wife of an elector of the Hapsburg empire, had said no and had whisked her daughter off to a hiding place.

After many complications, secret journeys (using the pseudonym Adolf Karlsson the King set off on a courtship mission to Germany) and diplomatic negotiations at the highest level, Maria Eleonora became the wife of Gustavus Adolphus and Queen of Sweden in 1620. The King was 25 and his queen 21. The

King's mother, Kristina, was appeased. Astrologers had predicted at the King's birth that he would wed at 25. The King would later call Maria Eleonora "my private tragedy". She never adjusted to Sweden's stark landscape, to the simpler ways of the Swedish court or to her role as mother to a crown princess, Kristina.

Appraisals of Maria Eleonora have differed. According to the Frenchman Charles Ogier, who met her several times in 1634, she was endearing, feminine and gifted. Ogier praised her for her knowledge of architecture, among other subjects. Maria Eleonora had a passion for castles and she activated a number of construction projects. None of her projects was realised.

The Chancellor, Axel Oxenstierna, was less enthusiastic about the Queen. He complained that he was forced to devote two days each week to the Queen's

Here at Kalmar Castle, Gustavus Adolphus broke off his journey to Germany to propose to Maria Eleonora of Brandenburg. The girl's mother had spirited her away to foil the courtship.

After many complications, Maria Eleonora became the bride of King Gustavus Adolphus. She received this regal diadem in 1620.

Gustavus Adolphus and Maria Eleonora had a daughter in 1623. She was christened Kristina but died in infancy. Her simple coffin is kept in Riddarholmen church in Stockholm.

In 1626, Maria Eleonora gave birth to a second daughter. She too was christened Kristina. In this portrait by Jacob Heinrich Elbfas she is eight years old.

Christina
Drottning til Sverige; Född d:8 Dec:
1626. Död d: 9 Apr: 1689.
504

The Swedish fleet gathered at Älvsnabben island in the south part of the Stockholm archipelago before sailing for Germany in 1630. From here, three-year-old Kristina waved goodbye to her father, Gustavus Adolphus. Mooring rings and fortifications from the time remain.

affairs. When the now-widowed Queen demanded that two royal councillors were to sit with Princess Kristina at her dinner table to serve her water, the Council took from the Queen her right to guardianship. Later, Maria Eleonora would find herself in what was tantamount to house arrest in Gripsholm castle.

A Swedish historian, Nils Ahnlund, gave a slightly different picture of the unhappy Queen. She had a warm, good heart and exceptionally good taste, said Ahnlund, but adds: "She had no control over her emotions and every enterprise she undertook needed supervision." In recent years, researchers in female history have provided a completely different explanation for Maria Eleonora's actions. In this version, the royal councillors, especially Axel Oxenstierna, saw the Queen as a power rival. They had a reason to slander her and portray her as an intellectually feeble hysteric. In fact, her sole desire was to be recognised as a queen with a queen's authority.

The Queen's strange behaviour after the death of Gustavus Adolphus was also explained by the feminists: not to want to bury your husband and to carry his embalmed heart on your person was in accordance with the customs of the time, as was her ordering of a coffin for two so she could rest with her beloved.

Maria Eleonora must have had a strong will and a firm conviction of her own importance. In 1640, she staged an escape of which no one thought her capable. Every month, the Queen used to fast for three days. In that period, she would be left alone in her rooms in Gripsholm castle, with her lady-in-waiting for sole company. In mid-July, she announced that this time, her fast would last six days. Her meagre fasting provisions were brought in and the Queen locked her door.

At one o'clock on the morning of 22 July, Maria Eleonora escaped through a window. Outside, her stable keeper and a Danish painter were waiting. The escapees made their way to the coast and a ship carried the Queen to the Danish Court. Later, she rejoined her family in Brandenburg. But after eight years in exile, she returned to Sweden. She died in 1655, shortly after the abdication of Queen Kristina. The most bitter denunciation of Maria Eleonora came from her own daughter. In Queen Kristina's unfinished autobiography, she wrote at length about her childhood and a mother who "could not stand me because I was a girl and because she found me ugly."

Kristina traced her mother's disappointment to Kristina's birth. Maria Eleonora had been pregnant three times before Kristina was born. High infant mortality afflicted even royalty and in 1621, a year after her wedding, the young queen had her first miscarriage. In 1623, she gave birth to a daughter who was christened Kristina but who died in infancy. In 1625, the Queen had another miscarriage, this time in an advanced stage of her pregnancy. The stillborn baby was a son. When Maria Eleonora was to give birth again in December 1626, expectations were therefore high. The court astrologers predicted a prince.

"I was born," wrote Kristina, "with a cowl covering all but my face, my arms and my legs. I had thick hair all over my body and cried with a strong, deep voice. All this led the midwives to believe I was a boy." The Queen never recovered from the shock of discovering that her son was a girl. The King found his own way to deal with the disappointment: he made the girl into a boy. "I hope," he said, "that this girl will be as good as a boy for me." Kristina became her father's tomboy.

When the King brought two-year-old Kristina to Kalmar castle in the south, the castle warden asked if the custom of firing a salute as the King approached might scare the little girl. "Fire away!" answered the King. "She is the daughter of a soldier and will have to get used to it."

When Kristina was three, Gustavus Adolphus embarked with the fleet for Germany to wage war against the German emperor. It was the last time father and daughter would see each other. The little one was left, waving and crying, on a rugged, grey rock in the Stockholm archipelago. She wrote in her memoirs that she cried so hard for three days she thought she would go blind. She wrote to her father in Germany: "I beg Your Majesty to remember me and to return soon and please to send me something pretty in the meantime." In her old age, Kristina recalled the time after her father's death with loathing. Maria Eleonora's sorrow was limitless and the relationship between mother and daughter worsened. Kristina was six and hated the dark palace where the Queen draped the rooms in black, from floor to ceiling. Heavy, black curtains hid the windows.

Kristina discovered great pleasure in reading and having discussions with her teachers. Her relaxation was in receiving foreign emissaries, no matter how for-

Princess Kristina was six years old in 1632 when she wrote in German to her father, the King, in Germany: "Return soon and please to send me something pretty in the meantime. I shall always be good."

The King's slippers are well-worn. The King was a great man but had small feet – approximately size 40 Euro or 7 USA.

Gnedigster herr vilgelieb-
ter herr vatter E K M
sein mein gehorsamen kindt-
lichen dinst vnd wünschen
von gott dem almechtigen
viller gesunder zeit, vnd [illegible] gethan
~~ders~~ ~~[illegible]~~ als [illegible] bitt E M
dochter zū trost balt wider komen
wollen auch was schö-
vnd mir auch [illegible] lob geschi-
cken, ich befleissige mich im lese
vnd [illegible]
wil alzeit wacker lernen,
vnd verbleib

E K M

gehorsame
dochter

Christina P S

Christina P S.

mal the occasion. "I remember how delighted I was," she wrote, "to see all these people at my feet and to have them kiss my hand." Two years after the King's death, a French nobleman, Count d'Avaux, visited the court: "The Queen was seated alone on a raised dias under a canopy. On our entrance, she arose and greeted each of us with a curtsy. The ambassador made the requisite three bows and stepped towards the throne, kissed the Queen's hand and gave his speech in Latin. While the ambassador was delivering his speech with great dignity and elegance, the Queen held him in her gaze, as though she understood."

At the time Count d'Avaux made his visit, Kristina was eight years old. She would become as famous as her great father: as regent, as convert, as remarkable woman in the centre of the Catholic universe. But we leave the child queen as the French count kisses her hand.

There were many stories about Queen Maria Eleonora's boundless sorrow on the death of her husband Gustavus Adolphus in 1632. One told of how she carried the King's embalmed heart with her constantly, in a little box. The linen cloth said to have been wrapped around the heart is preserved at the Royal Armoury in Stockholm.

Fairy-tale Kings and Fable Heroes

OLD WIVES' TALES, the Danes used to say, dismissing Sweden's glorious history as nonsense. Unfortunately, they were right. Sweden's ancient history, as recounted by Archbishop Johannes Magnus in his book *The History of All the Kings of the Geats and Sveas* is fable. What Johannes Magnus and the Geatish history writers of the 16th and 17th centuries claimed is nationalistic balderdash and over-eager interpretation of older source material. The stone-etched runes are not the world's oldest written letters. Magog, the grandson of Noah, did not journey to Sweden 88 years after the Flood. Nor did he become Sweden's first king. Mythological Atlantis was not located in the Nordic region. The Sveas and the Geats did not conquer parts of Africa and Asia, nor did they pose a threat to the pharaohs of Egypt and the emperors of Rome.

The Greek hero Hercules symbolises strength and courage and was often depicted in 17th-century art and decoration. He is to be found as both young and old on the Vasa.

What Johannes Magnus and others claimed is astonishing. What is even more astonishing is that it made up Sweden's official history for several hundred years. The weave of fables, myths and history that Johannes Magnus created borrowed threads from Norse mythology, classical Greek mythology, Roman history and the New and Old Testaments. The warp that held the weave together was Johannes Magnus's own imagination and his desire to create a place for Sweden in world history.

Hercules, clad in a lion pelt and bearing a club, stands on the roof of Stockholm's House of Nobility, built in the mid-17th century.

He succeeded. His book was written in Latin and was read throughout educated Europe. No other Swedish history has been spread nearly as widely.

More importantly, it gave Swedes enormous self-confidence. It was not with Bible in hand that they threw themselves into histrionic wars against rich countries such as Denmark, Poland, Russia – and finally, the mightiest nation in all of Europe, the Hapsburgian state led by the German emperor. The shield Swedes held before them was their nation's glorious history as told by Johannes Magnus.

His history influenced both great and small. Three examples: When Prince Erik became king in 1560, he was given the sequential number XIV. This was because there had been 13 Eriks among Johannes Magnus's 150 previous Swedish monarchs. When in 1611 Gustavus Adolphus's father, Karl IX, wanted to terminate the calamitous war against the Danes, he proposed a duel. Karl wrote to the Danish king, Kristian IV: "Let us, according to the customs and habits of the ancient Geats, meet in a duel on flat ground and without armour." But King Karl was scarcely in a condition to fight; by this time he was an old, sick man, barely able to talk. Kristian, on the other hand, was in his prime and riposted: "It would be healthier for Thee to keep Thee to the warmth of a tile oven rather than fence

with Us." When Gustavus II Adolphus was crowned king in 1617, the celebrations included a tournament. The King dressed up as King Berik, one of Johannes Magnus's fable kings. The choice was made with care. According to the chronicles, Berik had united the warring Geats and Sveas and turned them against the nation's foreign enemies. These, according to Berik, were to be found on the other side of the Baltic among Estonians, Livonians, Finns and Cours. The fictitious chronicle went on to relate how Berik successfully conquered lands to the east and south.

Gustavus Adolphus was a little over 20 when he put on Berik's armour. Four years later, he would unite the nation, just as the saga king, and sail his troops against Livonia, Poland and finally, in 1630, the emperor's Germany.

Gustavus Adolphus lived with fable kings and saga heroes. On the walls of his castles hung tapestries with motifs from Geatic history. When the King stayed at his castle in Kalmar, in the far south, he was stared at by Hercules, the hero of Greek mythology, from a ceiling painting. According to accounts, the painting was by Gustavus Adolphus's uncle, King Erik XIV. Geatish, Greek and Roman were all woven together. One of Berik's most terrifying warriors, so the story went, was the Amazon queen Penthesilea, who had also fought in the Trojan War.

Gustavus Adolphus was crowned king in 1617. A jousting tournament was arranged for the occasion. The King wore this suit of armour and represented the mythical King Berik. According to histories of the time, Berik united the Geats and Sveas and conquered large lands to the east.

In the ceiling painting, Hercules has his usual accessories: the lion pelt and a club. He had won the pelt by killing the Nemean lion in the first of his Twelve Labours. Hercules crushed the invincible animal to death with his bare hands, then skinned it with its own claws when no other tool could pierce the skin.

In the painting, Hercules looks slightly tired and worn-out, with his lion pelt tied in a fancy way around his hips. Nothing indicates which Labour he has just completed – perhaps the one the Roman poets called his most arduous: impregnating in one single night each of King Thespius's fifty daughters.

Johannes Magnus's history gave inspiration to more than just the King and the nation's leaders. His chronicle was translated into Swedish from Latin and published in the 1620s in an affordable version. When the King's secretary, Peder Eriksson, travelled the land to raise funds for the war against Poland, he held fiery speeches based on accounts of Berik's glorious wars. Money poured in: whether this was due to the speeches or to the fact that Eriksson was offering 14 per cent interest is unclear. But the aim was to permeate the entire population with the same courage, strength and sacrificial resolve as the Geats and the ancient heroes.

On his appointment as professor of history at the University of Uppsala in 1627, Johannes Loccenius analysed the role of history. It should preserve for posterity the deeds of heroes, he said, but more importantly should illuminate "the

Stockholm's most skilful wood sculptor in the 1620s was Mårten Redtmer. He fashioned the most expressive sculptures on the Vasa and did much work elsewhere, including the decorations for the cathedral's organ. The organ has since been moved to Bälinge church, north of Stockholm. The small pictures on this page and the spread on the next page are of that organ.

The grotesque mask opposite decorates an organ in Övertorneå church in northern Sweden. It was sculpted by Mårten Redtmer and strongly resembles masks found on the Vasa.

examples of famous men". The Government Archives had been founded in 1618 charged with preserving letters, documents – in fact, everything written that described the feats of Swedish heroes. Sweden's National Heritage Board is therefore the world's oldest such institution. It was founded in 1630 to save Geatic relics, etched in rock, built of stone or formed of flint, wood, bronze, iron, silver or gold.

The most exceptional example of how fables, sayings and myths were incorporated into both art and military art, and into power and glory is, however, the warship Vasa. The Vasa can be described as the prime example of the fondness that existed in Sweden's era as a Great Power for massive, spectacular, over-loaded and unique constructions.

Later, by the mid-1600s, the Swedish aristocracy completely absorbed the European habit of squandering for its own sake. This was a time of orgies in building, food and drink, costumes and parties. Squandering was a way of demonstrat-

Two life-size warriors stand guard on either side of the Vasa dynasty's coat of arms on the Vasa's stern. They are clad in 17th-century armour.

The preserved tools of a 17th-century wood carver.

ing that one could afford to lavish money on temporal things – even if the money was not there. Squandering gave renown. Economic prudence was a bad thing.

But in the 1620s, this ritual spending had yet to mature. There was the magnificent history and the similarly sized ambitions, but Sweden was still too poor. Stockholm was a little shanty town where goats grazed on sod-sown roofs. And the country's other towns were "bereft of commerce, rotten and dilapidated" according to a drastic statement by the King. None of the beautiful and extravagantly furnished castles and palaces had yet been built. Skokloster, Ulriksdal, Venngarn, Läckö and Makalös were all built decades later. Large parts of Stockholm were in ashes after the catastrophic fire of 1625.

At that very time, only months after that terrible fire, construction of the Vasa was started. Frames were erected, planks were shaped and sculptures depicting heroes from all ages and cultures were carved. Like a Phoenix, the warship Vasa arose from the ashes of Stockholm. The Vasa was to be a man-of-war with many cannons and heavy firepower, but even through its luxury and in its figurative design, it would promote Sweden's reputation abroad. From a military standpoint, it was ludicrous to put five hundred heavy sculptures on a warship and smother it with gilt, indigo, Spanish green and red lead. The Vasa would have been a more stable vessel without all this ornamentation.

According to legend, King Erik XIV himself painted the ceiling of a hall at Kalmar castle. The painting shows a rather tired Hercules with club and lion pelt.

But if the object was to portray a powerful nation, its proud history and its strong and wise king, the decoration filled a real function. And, in the mid-1620s, this was indeed more important than much else. Therefore, Geatic kings – perhaps one of them Berik himself – stand guard by the Vasa dynasty's coat of arms on the ship's stern. Therefore, King David is to be seen playing the harp. Therefore, biblical hero and God's executor Gideon is there, blowing his horn and chasing off enemies. Gideon, incidentally, was the King's code name in secret correspondence between Sweden and Germany. And therefore, under the bowsprit, Roman emperors parade alongside their names. Only one emperor is missing: Augustus, Gustavus Adolphus's favourite. Gustavus and Augustus are strikingly similar names and Gustavus Adolphus was at times called the Swedish Augustus.

The young King himself – perhaps a symbolic Augustus – is to be found at the top of the stern. Underneath is written "GARS" – Gustavus Adolphus Rex Sueciae, Gustavus Adolphus King of Sweden. The King put much importance on the decoration of the Vasa. The number of wood-carvers at the Skeppsgården shipyard in Stockholm increased constantly throughout the 1620s. The best-known and best paid of them was Mårten Redtmer. His wage is a good indication of the importance placed on his work. Master Mårten had his own farm property and a very decent wage: in 1626 he was paid 354 *daler* – as much as a naval officer. Master Mårten's sculptures were the best and most valuable on the Vasa: the royal coat of arms, the figurehead lion and Hercules.

Among war spoils brought back from Prague in 1648 by the Swedish army was this large statue of Hercules. Today it stands in the park outside the Royal Family's residence at Drottningholm Palace, outside Stockholm.

There are two versions of the King's beloved Hercules: the virile youth and the wise old man. The young Hercules has his lion pelt and club, just as on the ceiling of Kalmar castle, but his pelt is thrown rakishly over his shoulder, not prudishly tied round his waist. The older Hercules has Cerberus, the guard dog of Hades, chained at his feet. Fetching the beast from the Underworld and then leading it down again was the hero's twelfth and last Labour. Which of the two Hercules figures the King preferred to identify himself with we leave unsaid. When construction of the Vasa started, the King was 31 years old and had recently become a father.

The sculptures on the Vasa were originally painted in vivid colours.

INSIGHT AND PERSPECTIVE

The Swedes were neither travellers nor explorers nor colonists. Not like the Dutch, the English, the Spanish, the Portuguese, the French and the Italians. Those people sailed the world, trading and conquering new countries and riches. Sweden rarely aimed beyond the Baltic.

'Only cranes pass through countries without growing wiser.'

Wild Geese, Cranes and Other Travellers

ONLY CRANES AND wild geese pass through countries without growing wiser, wrote the wise Per Brahe *père* four hundred years ago. But Swedes were not travellers, nor explorers nor colonists, like the Dutch, English, Spanish, Portuguese and Italians. Sweden's few modest colonial adventures in the mid-17th century lasted only a few years. New Sweden on the Delaware River in North America was bought from the Indians in 1638 and conquered by the Dutch in 1655. There was a small, fortified Swedish trading post for less than ten years at Cabo Corso on the West African coast. It was taken by a Danish privateer in 1658 and quickly sold to the Dutch.

Educational journeys made by Swedes in the early 1600s seldom went further than Germany and Holland. The travellers were mostly young noblemen and students. A trip could last up to two or three years and was often motivated by a desire to learn new languages, principally French and Latin – German was already almost a mother tongue. Studies at northern European universities also included jurisprudence, constitutional law and politics.

There were many temptations and dangers for young students. A watercolour in a diary from the beginning of the 17th century shows how young aristocrats

Travellers returned with exotic souvenirs. This ostrich egg with its handsome engraving is part of the 17th century art collection at Skokloster palace.

The Church of St. Peter in Rome, centre of the feared Catholic church, was built in the first half of the 17th century and is thus contemporary with the Vasa.

might pass their time while sojourning in foreign countries. Dressed in the latest styles, a group sits by a gaming table. Cards are thrown on the table and those not in the game are fondling several young women. The background shows a glimpse of a hilly countryside, so this house of pleasure may have been in south Germany. A youth pounds at the door, anxious to partake of the pleasures within. He has a rapier at his side and pointed spurs on his high boots. He seems to be in a mild frenzy since a pack of small dogs is nipping at his heels.

After copper and iron, tar and pitch were Sweden's biggest exports. Fifteen tall trees were needed to produce one barrel of tar. (next pages)

For Swedish travellers, London's social whirl was a revelation. Theatre was integral and Shakespeare was already widely published. This luxury edition from the 1630s was donated to the Royal Library by Sweden's present monarch, Carl XVI Gustaf.

Diaries and letters tell of travel and studies abroad. The inkwell, quill and writing case were a gift to the Swedish King in 1632.

But the greatest danger facing a young, Lutheran student was the heresies of the Catholics and Calvinists. To talk or mix with papists, either at home in Sweden or abroad, was politically risky. In 1624, three people in Stockholm were charged with harbouring Catholic sympathies and were executed.

Consequently, Sweden's cultural interchange with the Catholic parts of Europe all but ceased, and the continental influences that reached this northern country were filtered through northern Germany, Holland and England. The underlying reason was a fear of Jesuit machinations and Catholic counter-reformation. It was forbidden for those others than the nobility to visit Catholic universities until the mid-17th century.

An early Swedish voyager was Axel Oxenstierna, the man who was to become chancellor and one of the most powerful men not only in Sweden but in all of Europe, and who was described by the Pope himself as "one of the most brilliant

Mr. WILLIAM
SHAKESPEARES
COMEDIES,
HISTORIES, and
TRAGEDIES.
Published according to the true Originall Copies.
The second Impression.
Martin Droeshout sculpsit London
LONDON,
Printed by Tho. Cotes, for Robert Allot, and are to be sold at the signe
of the Blacke Beare in Pauls Church-yard. 1632.

men the world has yet seen". In 1599, Oxenstierna left Sweden for a study trip that would last four years. Axel was all of 16 years old and was accompanied by his two younger brothers, Gabriel and Krister. Not long into the journey, Krister fell ill and returned home.

The Oxenstierna brothers' journey was typical of the "travel madness" that afflicted young aristocrats, as their frumpish, older countrymen saw it. The journey was both business and pleasure, and young Axel was forced to pawn his collection of books in Stralsund, the north German port city, to be able to afford his ticket home.

The Sweden they left behind was an old-fashioned, almost mediaeval country. The population of Sweden proper was 850,000. Sweden's eastern part, Finland, had another 350,000 and Swedish Estonia 100,000. But only a small percentage lived in urban areas and Swedish towns were, as King Gustavus Adolphus would describe them later, "rotten, boring and decrepit". The country's natural resources, mainly iron, copper and silver, were poorly exploited and export income was modest.

Besides, enemies who took every chance to raid and provoke war traditionally surrounded Sweden: Denmark, Poland and Russia. Geographically, Sweden was enclosed in the Baltic, with only a small breathing hole to the west at the Älvsborg fortress – modern Gothenburg. Denmark ruled the four southernmost provinces of modern Sweden: Skåne, Blekinge, Bohuslän and Halland.

Fifty years later, the Baltic was virtually a Swedish inland sea, and Sweden had taken those four provinces. In addition, Sweden controlled territory near Bremen and Verden in Germany and Norway was cut in half by Swedish-controlled Trondheim.

But we are still in the 16th century, and the Oxenstierna brothers' first stop on their journey was Copenhagen. This was a major city, the like of which they had never seen and was not to be found in Sweden. At the time, Stockholm had a population of less than 10,000 and its buildings resembled peasant cottages, according to a foreign visitor. In Copenhagen, they saw broad, paved streets and met Continental culture – and a small colony of expatriate Swedes, there because of their opposition to the Swedish king. This was the year 1599 when Duke Karl seized power in Sweden by overthrowing the Catholic king, Sigismund.

Copenhagen duly impressed the young travellers but they took little notice of the exiled Swedes' cause. The Oxenstierna brothers were faithful supporters of Duke Karl. They soon journeyed on to the university at Rostock, where they spent a year.

That year was, as historian Nils Ahnlund writes, "a period of transition and preparation" for Axel Oxenstierna. This meant light studying and a lively social life. Life in this northern German university town could be both merry and vigorous. It was here that the young Danish astronomer, Tycho Brahe, had lost half his nose in a duel a few years earlier.

In Rostock, the Oxenstierna brothers met Jonas Rothovius. He was 27 years old and a student from farming stock in Småland. He accompanied the brothers as they journeyed on into Germany. Axel Oxenstierna's friendship with the farmer's son was later to become significant for the chancellor's knowledge of and understanding for the lower estates in Sweden.

From Rostock, the three youths travelled south to the famous university at Wittenberg. There they studied theology and other subjects. Jonas Rothovius wrote in a poem: "Noble Axel: each day, each night, you turn so scrupulously the Bible's holy pages." The holy pages "noble Axel" was reading were naturally being

A 17th-century souvenir from Bethlehem and the Holy Land.

Tulips were hard currency in Holland in the 1620s and 1630s and there was feverish speculation in bulb trading. One tulip bulb was sold in 1625 for 3,000 gold florins, twenty times the average annual wage.

In 1628, the year the Vasa sank, a young Rembrandt was at work in a studio in Leiden and painted this self-portrait.

interpreted according to pure Lutheran doctrine, even though Wittenberg was dangerously close to the border of Catholic southern Europe. As an 18-year-old, Axel Oxenstierna submitted a doctorate, defending a thesis on the doctrines of Catholicism.

Fear of the papists was so strong that it was not until a year later that Axel dared visit "enemy territory". By then the three had completed their studies and spent a half-year travelling in southern Germany. They visited Jesuits in Würzburg and the Calvinist Reformists in Heidelberg. "Men filled with delusion," was their verdict.

The three youths were more than just critical observers; they discovered that wine was cheap in Basel and many other useful facts. They found Strasbourg on the Rhine the most beautiful town of all. They did not visit any of the real European metropolises. Paris, London, Naples, Venice, Milan and Constantinople all had over a hundred thousand inhabitants by this time.

If the Oxenstierna brothers had made their trip a few years later, Holland would have been a must. In the beginning of the 17th century, Amsterdam was Europe's most expansive city. The Dutch East India Company was formed in 1602 and through it, the tiny country founded colonies and trading posts through-

out the world, out-doing Spain, Portugal, France and Italy in trade and shipping.

Amsterdam's canal system provided a template for town planners in the most diverse parts of the world. Gothenburg was planned in 1621 using the Dutch city as a model. The same was true for New York, or New Amsterdam as it was then called, and Batavia, now Jakarta.

Holland so dominated trade, culture and education that Swedes flocked there to study everything from the tulip trade to shipbuilding, and naturally traditional university subjects such as theology, philosophy, languages and politics. It is believed that eight hundred Swedes studied at the university in Leiden during the 17th century. Almost all Swedish teachers from Sweden's age as a Great Power were themselves educated in Holland.

The only Swede known to have made a longer journey in the early 1600s was Axel's cousin, Bengt Oxenstierna, later to be honoured with the nickname Traveller Bengt. He was born in 1591 at Frösvik Manor, close to Stockholm, and began his travels with a similar study trip to Germany as a 16-year-old. But instead of returning after a year, he continued to Venice.

"Venice," he wrote, "is the most beauteous and powerful city and may well be called a wonder of the world." He was captivated by the city's 8,000 gondolas, 400 bridges and the commedia dell'arte performances on St. Mark's Square and other

"A wonder of the world," marvelled Bengt Oxenstierna on seeing Venice. He visited the city in the beginning of the 17th century and admired its 8,000 gondolas. Building of the baroque church of Santa Maria Della Salute on the Grand Canal started in 1630.

Baroque art loved transforming odd-shaped shells and other natural objects into beautiful objets d'art. The patterning on this nautilus shell was done in Holland.

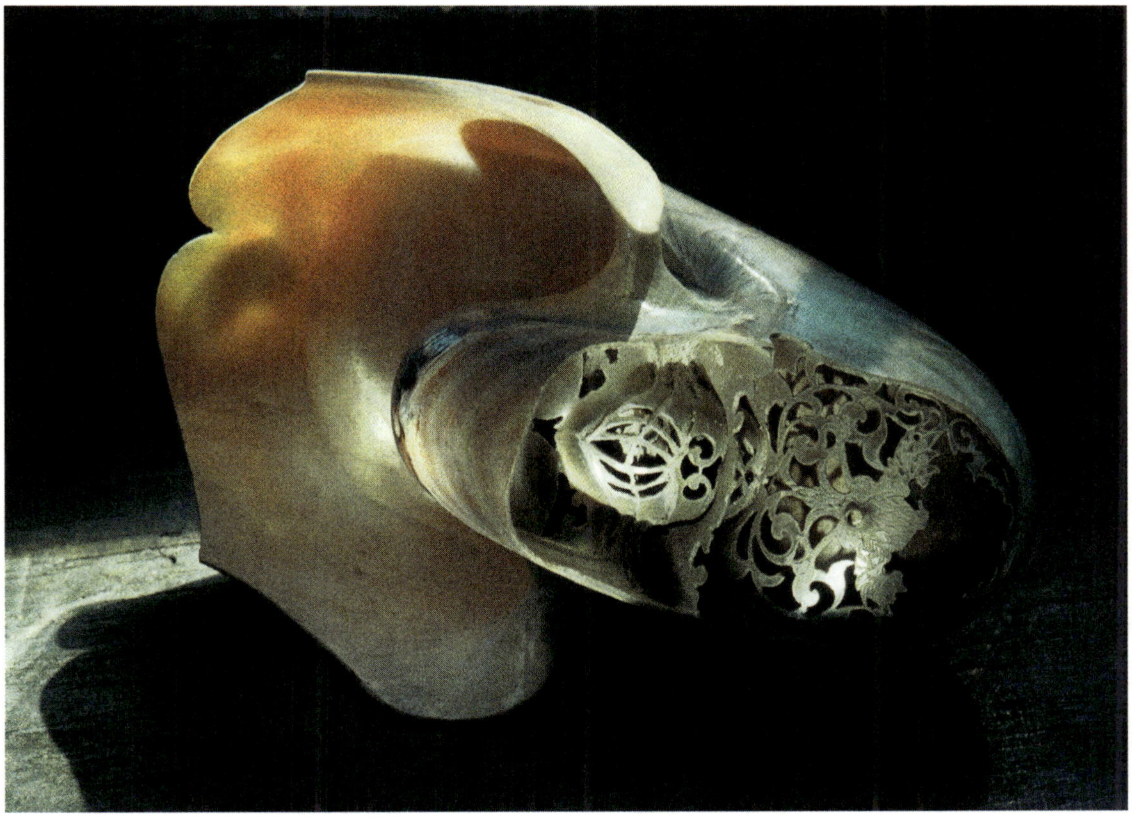

In the early 17th century, Holland was the world's greatest trading and maritime nation. Dutch cities swelled and culture flourished. One of the best-preserved cities of that time is Hoorn, with its symbolic ship on a church steeple.

In March 1610, Swedish general Jakob De la Gardie marched into Moscow and the Kremlin. His mission was to support Czar Vasilij IV against the Poles. But success was short-lived.

squares. But the greatest attraction was the shipyard and arsenal, storing 60,000 suits of armour and 250 galley ships, reported Traveller Bengt: "In a single room, eighty old prisoners-of-war sat patching sails."

From Venice, Bengt Oxenstierna continued to Jerusalem and points further east. Unfortunately, his notes have been lost and only fragments of his journey are known. There were, however, many adventures: he was captured by bandits and transported, wounded, to Cyprus; served as a soldier under the Duke of Tuscany; sailed to Constantinople, then Europe's biggest city; and continued through Asia Minor to Aleppo in Syria.

There, as a letter to his sister in Sweden reveals, he ran out of money. But the adventurer continued, taking "forty long days" to reach Baghdad, and on to Isfahan, the Persian capital. No Swede had ever travelled this far before. He took part in a war against the Turks, fighting on the side of Abbas the Great and remaining at his court for a full year.

When the grateful shah wanted to show the stranger the most valuable plant in his garden, Bengt told him that "in Sweden, the forests and hills are full of such bushes". The plant was the juniper, planted by Abbas by his golden fence.

"Traveller" Bengt Oxenstierna told King Gustavus Adolphus stories of Abbas the Great and the horticultural artistry of the Orient. The flowerbeds and plants at Kyoto's Katsura Imperial Palace date from that time.

In 1620, Traveller Bengt returned to Sweden and became one of King Gustavus Adolphus's closest men. As Master of the Horse he was part of the King's inner circle and followed him to Germany in 1630 when Sweden intervened in the Thirty Years' War. The King is said to have been greatly entertained by Traveller Bengt's stories and enjoyed relaxing while hearing about the juniper bushes of Abbas the Great, the sail-makers of Venice and the bandits in the Holy Land.

By this time, tens of thousands of Swedish farm boys had also come into contact with foreign lands and cultures. "Swedes learned their geography while marching," wrote the historian and author Erik Gustaf Geijer. The great Swedish armies that fought and plundered in Russia, Poland, the Baltic states and Germany during the Thirty Years' War both saw and conquered. Those who came home – and their number was frightening small – brought with them impressions of foreign countries and their cultures. Horizons are broadened even by military campaigns.

rboeden
Galge
rde
k
Lustholm
Raedholm

WHERE SHIPS ALMOST BRUSH THE HOUSES

Sweden was an inconsequential and poor country in the north with an inconsequential and poor capital. Stockholm's houses looked like Russian cottages, noted a surprised foreign traveller. Long nights, narrow streets, inns and impoverishment made the town dangerous to live in.

A Green Capital

PENNY KNAVE! screamed Anders in fury. "Kiss a mare between her legs!" The fight was on. Matz got a beer tankard in the head and two cuts. Göran fielded a haymaker to his ear but could still head-butt Anders from Torneå, bringing him down. Staffan Rolofson, the tax collector, seized the opportunity to make a run for it.

Staffan the Bailiff was the cause of the fisticuffs on Stockholm's Södermalm district that day in February 1626. In his capacity as royal official, he had knocked on the door of Burgher Erik Mattson to see whether his tax had been paid. So far so good, but Anders from Torneå "lost all reason" as he later told the court and tried to attack the "penny knave".

That fight indicated how tense the atmosphere was in Stockholm in the mid-1620s. More taxes, more conscription, more tariffs, disease, beer, schnapps and poverty often pushed the relationship between the King's officials and the townsfolk almost to breaking point.

In February 1623, the city's craftsmen flocked to Stortorget Square. There, they hurled abuse at the mayor, Hans Nilsson. He was known as Hans the Sausage or, pejoratively, the schnapps merchant or the sausage seller. Chasing off the guard, the irate craftsmen held the mayor prisoner for a short while. There were dire ramifications; some of the rebels were condemned to death and executed. Merely abusing the mayor was enough to earn a sentence of death. Anders from Torneå was also sentenced to death three years later for his deeds, even though neither king nor excise officer came to harm. However, the sentence was never carried out and Anders was freed by the court of appeal.

The Three Crowns royal palace dominated Stockholm for the first decades of the 17th century. Tall, imposing and old, it rose above a town otherwise made up of wooden shacks and the occasional stone building. In the palace, the King held sway with his council and his officials – when they were there. Stockholm was a dirty, odorous, unhealthy hole and, at times, dangerous. The King and the other aristocrats often preferred to stay in their palaces and properties in the provinces. This was before the age of the great urban mansions. "Stockholm looks so green," wrote an astonished Dutchman, Anthonis Goeteeris. He was used to the magnificent stone buildings of continental Europe and confronted a town with rooftops covered with bark and grass sod, where goats jumped from roof to roof, looking for the juiciest tussocks.

Stockholm had a population of ten thousand people, two thousand hogs, one

Stockholm is green, observed an astonished Dutchman, Anthonis Goeteeris, on a visit to the Swedish capital in the first years of the 17th century. The houses had sod roofs and vegetable gardens, and cattle were grazing everywhere. An old species of cabbage now grows in the garden by Stockholm's Vasa Museum.

Stockholm in the early 17th century. The Three Crowns palace dominated the present Old Town island; the trading houses and nobles' mansions were yet to be built. *(next pages)*

thousand cows and at least as many goats and chickens as people. The streets were narrow and twisted and indescribably filthy. Sweden had a capital with houses reminiscent of Russian peasant dwellings, commented Anthonis, who was both amused and bemused: "One does not know what to make of it!"

Diplomats and nobles visiting the capital had to lodge in common inns such as The Three Barrels, The Four Rummers, The Golden Sun, The Rose Garland and The Kikendal. There, drunken seamen and girls of dubious character did their best to separate the strangers from their money.

None of the handsome buildings that today make up the Old Town's façade facing the harbour was yet built. Around the main island ran the town wall, broken in parts by narrow streets accessing the all-important quay, for Stockholm was no longer a fortified town. When the King was to receive the keys of the city in 16 14 he found the symbolic ceremony unnecessary. The city wall, the gates and the fortifications had all become obsolete. The keys could just as well be in the keeping of the city's burghers. A hundred years earlier, King Gustav Vasa had realised that strategically, the adjacent archipelago with its islands, skerries and reefs represented far better fortification than a town wall. There are only two narrow sea channels into the city, and both were easy to block, forcing friend and foe to enter or leave between narrow embankments. From that time, the city's defence forces were encamped there.

The great mansions of the nobility were built in the mid-1600s. Chancellor Axel Oxenstierna's handsome house, begun in 1653, has the cathedral and the royal palace as neighbours.

Stockholm's importance was as a harbour and a naval shipyard. Travellers were horrified at the poverty and filth but still found praise for the harbour. Nowhere else was there a safer, more secure harbour, noted the Frenchman Charles Ogier when he came to Stockholm in the early 1630s. "The largest, most deep-draughted ships can sail so close to the town as to almost brush the houses." The last observation was naturally an exaggeration but Stockholm's importance at that time as a shipyard and equipping station for the navy cannot be overstated.

Alongside the Three Crowns palace and the churches, the royal bakery on Norrmalm, or the Northern Mainland, was one of the city's biggest buildings. This was characteristic: most of the ten thousand inhabitants had some connection with the fleet, since Stockholm was primarily a naval base where ships were built and equipped. Bakers, brewers and butchers belonged to the trades which grew most in the early 1600s. Their principal source of income was the navy, which they supplied with bread, beer, beef and pork. The fleet was frequently at sea from May to November and the large crews needed tens of thousands of barrels of salt beef and salt pork, loaves of bread, and beer.

In the Norrmalm district and close to the naval shipyard were stores and workshops for the navy's needs. The seamen who crewed the King's ships lived in small dwellings in both Norrmalm and Södermalm. Gun carriages were assembled at a workshop where the Foreign Ministry now stands on Gustav Adolf Square. Rope was made in a long ropewalk in Humlegården park. The royal bakery, where flat rye cakes were baked then stacked in barrels, still stands in Norrmalm. Still there, too, are innumerable oak chips from the logs that were fashioned into planking, frames and curved pieces for warships. The chips turn up whenever construction workers dig on the islet known as Blasieholmen, where the shipyard lay.

At the time when Anders from Torneå smashed a beer tankard onto the head of his antagonist in Södermalm in early 1626, much of the Old Town's main island had been burned to the ground. On the evening of 1st September 1625 two women were brewing beer in a house not far from where the House of the Nobility now stands. At ten in the evening, the tower watchman in the cathedral sounded the alarm: Fire!

There was an evening breeze from the west and the flames leapt from roof to roof, spreading quickly along the southern and western parts of the Old Town. The winter supplies of firewood, stacked along the house walls, fed the flames.

The governor of Stockholm, Klas Horn, described the scene in a letter: "When the populace had taken to their beds, a strident fire began in a brewery to the

The navigable channels leading to Stockholm harbour snake around islands and through narrow straits. At Dalarö island, a fortlet guards access to the capital. Building on it started in 1623.

Riddarholm church in Stockholm. (next pages)

Net-gathering in a church mural from the 17th century. Islanders from the archipelago sailed or rowed to the capital with food and other saleable items. Most in demand were fish, wild fowl, eggs and firewood.

west. Houses and sheds were filled with firewood, and when the fire approached, it danced around so one scarcely knew what to do."

Swedish soldiers and German seamen helped put the fires out, throwing wet sails over the roofs. It did not help much. Navy seamen in Södermalm were alerted and ran down to the town, not to help in the firefighting but to save the warships moored below the palace, ready to load cannonballs, cannon and gunpowder. The boatswains dragged the ships to safety and moored them close to where the Vasa was to founder three years later.

The Three Crowns palace was spared – this time. So, too, was the relatively new German Church. Flames licked at it twice but were extinguished. The small dwellings to the southwest were, however, devastated. It was a catastrophe for the house-owners, but it provided the King with an excuse for a total renovation of the capital. In a few decades, the town was completely changed. Stockholm had to improve and be "populated," in the words of the Chancellor, Axel Oxenstierna. He believed that if Sweden was to be a Great Power, it must have a capital worthy of a great power. This excluded winding alleys and streets with no end. Great

Fighting fires was difficult, if not impossible. The fire extinguishers of the time resembled long-legged insects. Fire pumps and a large number of other tools from the time can be seen at Skokloster, the best preserved of Sweden's 17th-century palaces.

An Italian traveller, Magalotti, made a drawing of a typical Swedish inn.

Power nobles must be able to journey in their coach-and-twos. Were the streets less serpentine and dirty, there would be no reason for people to be carried around in sedan chairs.

This provided a motive for the transformation of Stockholm into an exemplary baroque city, with straight streets and square blocks. The city's first boulevard started from the point where the fire had begun. It was broad and straight and named King's Street (today: Stora Nygatan). Chancellor Axel Oxenstierna bought a piece of real estate to build a mansion on. It was never built. The spot is now occupied by the House of the Nobles, where building began in 1641.

The history of the fire of 1625 can be seen in the town plan for the Old Town: in the northeast part, which the fire did not ravage, the streets are still narrow and twisting. The west has a more regular street network, in true baroque style.

Far from all of Stockholm's streets were laid with cobblestones. Dirty, muddy paths were more common. Foreign visitors complained that it was difficult and uncomfortable to travel properly, by horse and carriage. It was in fact impossible on some of the muddier tracks.

The transformation of the city had thus begun when Gustavus Adolphus sailed off to attack Germany in 1630. And there was more than a pious wish in his farewell speech to the burghers when he expressed the hope that "your small huts may become great stone houses, your small boats large ships".

The changes took only a few decades but were still incomplete when the King's corpse was brought back to the capital in 1634. The funeral procession passed along the new, wide Kungsgatan or King's Street, but the last part was through the narrow, mediaeval Västerlånggatan. It was still bordered by walls blackened by the fire. To honour the King, the walls had been whitewashed. Black cloth covered the dirty street. Sweden's transformation from mediaeval nation of peasants to European Great Power had begun but was far from complete. There was much to hide from the procession.

The cloth from Västerlånggatan was later used to clothe the poorly equipped soldiers stationed in Karelia, "who go naked and have been without clothes since their general last was there".

The Whoremonger of The Black Dog

THE EMBROIDERY shows Jesus Christ's parable of the Prodigal Son, but is instead a grotesque depiction of Swedish drinking habits and life in the countless inns of Stockholm in the early 17th century. A young gentleman is raising his glass, but has already had too much to drink. A dog licks up his vomit. At the same time, a seductive young woman is making advances.

Full of lust, she has turned to him, strumming on a lute. The lady innkeeper is spying on them through the kitchen hatch. She has a pleased smile on her face and winks at the kitchen boy who is carefully noting the number of glasses and pots with chalk and a black slate. The young gentleman is on credit and the moral of the scene is written on the top edge of the embroidery: "His purse will soon be emptied."

Morals were at a low level in Sweden at this time. People drank, fought and fornicated. "Let the pitcher do its rounds and bring on the naked maids," bellowed an old vicar who had invited the Frenchman Ogier to dinner. Ogier was a cultivated person from the continent and was both shocked and repelled. He was struck constantly by the barbaric drinking habits of the Swedes. The cup and the Bible are always side by side on the table, he complained on seeing an eight-year-old child, intoxicated by beer, slumbering over an opened bible. In Sweden, they do not drink of thirst or for the taste of it, he reflected. In this country, the idea is to drink your guests under the table.

These habits belonged not only to peasants and vulgar people but also to men

The inns in Stockholm were numerous and beer flowed. Court records from the time tell of fights and killings. The drinking horn dates from the early 17th century.

The embroidery relates both the parable of the Prodigal Son and also depicts a Swedish inn scene of four hundred years ago.

otherwise admired. When Ogier travelled on, he summed up what he had seen: "The Swedes drink too much and eat food that is too badly prepared."

The King drank wine, confirms his daughter Kristina in writing of her life, but she added that he never drank so much that he forgot his honour and his duties. "Drinking is a common fault in the Nordic countries," she noted.

The King and his closest retinue drank Rhenish wine. The courtiers had to make do with French. The common people drank beer. The quantities were enormous. When Dutchman Anthonis Goeteeries visited Gustavus Adolphus, drinking was so intense that the guest was forced to lift the tablecloth, poke his fingers down his throat and vomit under the table. He wiped his mouth on the cloth, composed himself quickly and was able to continue drinking as if nothing had happened.

In simpler inns, food was served on ceramic or wooden plates or in wooden bowls. These lead-glazed ceramic bowls were found on board the Vasa. More exclusive services were of pewter.

And everyone drank, everywhere. Whenever the lunatics, old and infirm at Danvikens hospital in Stockholm got their hands on money, they spent it immediately on beer and schnapps. This has got to stop, admonished the hospital management in 1626. Money should be spent on shirts, shoes, cloth and soap.

It is unusual that soap was mentioned. The 17th century was a dirty one. There was deep suspicion against water and cleanliness since water, like air, was believed

to spread disease – a quite correct observation in itself. King Louis XIV of France was said to have bathed only twice in his life and became ill both times.

The squalor of the towns was awful. The stink of excrement from people and animals mixed with that of stagnant water, rotting food, smoke and tar, drying fish and mud. At the same time, Stockholmers loved public and private bathing. The children at the orphanage on Riddarholmen island who sewed navy uniforms were allowed to bathe every Saturday afternoon, when they were given a fresh set of clothes. They were given clean sheets every fortnight.

Stockholm had a number of public bathhouses and an unknown number of illegal ones. There was official encouragement to frequent the public bathhouses, for both hygienic and moral reasons, but foreign visitors were horrified over the lightly dressed girls paid to whip the male bathers to provoke a healthy sweat.

This was not the custom on the continent. There, most of these establishments had been closed down for public health reasons. Bathhouses were often brothels under another name and the new disease, syphilis, had spread across Europe at lightning speed. It had come from America at the end of the 15th century. Captain Vicente Pinzón on the Niña in Columbus's little fleet went to see a doctor shortly after their successful return to the port of Palos on 15 March 1493. Doctor Ruy

Drinking vessels were made of thin wooden staves, bound with pliable willow. The technique was called casking and was used for both barrels and smaller kegs, and – as here – for beer tankards.

Inns of the time could be both enjoyable and dangerous. Fights were common and the women who ran many of the inns had to be brusque with their guests. This 17th-century painting shows an inn in the province of Skåne. (next pages)

Diaz de Isla correctly diagnosed the red blotches on Captain Pinzón's skin and mucous membranes, although the disease was not to get a name for another fifty years.

The man who found a name for the epidemic venereal disease was a Veronese doctor, Girolamo Fracastoro. He described in verse his theory of how the disease came to Earth. One hot, dry summer, a shepherd called Syphilus built an altar to his king instead of to the sun god who had ravaged all green vegetation. The sun god punished Syphilus by afflicting him with a disease that gave him a thousand small sores. The poem was "Syphilis Sive Morbus Gallicus," and was no literary masterpiece. The writer almost certainly took the name Syphilus from Ovid's *Metamorphoses*, where one of Niobe's seven sons bore it.

Columbus's ships were carrying not only six Indians, gold and birds and mammals that had never been seen previously; a large part of the crew was also infected with syphilis, a disease that had not existed in the Old World in this form.

Women emptied the town's latrines. It was judged a suitable punishment for prostitutes. From a contemporary drawing.

Soldiers and sailors quickly spread the disease across Europe and the hotbeds of infection that the bathhouses represented were closed down. As usual, Sweden was about a half a century behind, and both legal and illegal bathhouses were doing good trade in Stockholm at the outset of the 17th century. Just as on the continent, the illegal ones were largely disguised brothels.

If all the whores from Södermalm turned up, said a prostitute under interrogation at the court in Norrmalm, they wouldn't fit in this room. Fraud and trickery flourished around the illegal bathhouses. A popular ruse was stealing a customer's clothes – and then selling them back. Both customers and prostitutes could be hit. Herman Dankwart and Margareta the Fish lost their clothes "as they lay a-bed". The thief turned out to be the city's executioner.

Fistfights, knife fights and use of the rapier were common. Darkness protected those afraid of the light and, in winter, Stockholm was pitch-dark for most of the day, providing opportunities for many. A hand lantern could be smashed, rendering victims helpless. Money, clothes and weapons changed ownership. In 1624 and 1625, sixteen murders were committed in Stockholm, a city of only about ten thousand inhabitants.

Naval seamen were often in trouble. When osteologist Ebba During examined the 25 skeletons found on the Vasa, she saw that a third of them had injuries: broken legs and noses and fractured jaws. They were probably not war injuries, since Swedes were rarely involved in battles at sea in those days. They were, far more likely, souvenirs of street fights and fights in inns.

There was a price list for the most common injuries. To inflict a broken finger

cost three marks. A cut on the hand or a punch to the ear cost the same. Giving someone an ugly head wound or chopping off a hand was worth twenty marks.

Winter darkness was dense, pierced only by tallow candles and train oil lamps. A street mugging often began by the perpetrator smashing his victim's lamp, plunging the scene into darkness.

An individual who often appeared in court records in the 1620s was a Thomas the Dancer. He was a seaman on The Black Dog, but seems to have been occupied mainly in robbery and seduction.

According to a court record from 7 February 1625, he was born in the northern part of the Stockholm archipelago. The record shows that he was accused of stealing two barrels of malt. His punishment was to run the gauntlet. The next year, he was in trouble again. This time, he accused a former girlfriend of having stolen a necklace. She was imprisoned but set free when it turned out that he had slept with her and promised to marry her if she became pregnant.

In early August 1628, Thomas the Dancer was arrested again and sent to jail. He had broken into a boat and stolen a pot of food, ten coins, two tin plates, a little kettle and a psalm book. The stolen goods were found in his home. Only a few weeks later, he was in the court record again. In the intervening period, he

Hops were an important crop.

One of the chests found onboard the Vasa had a complex combination lock. Even a common seaman needed to protect his simple belongings.

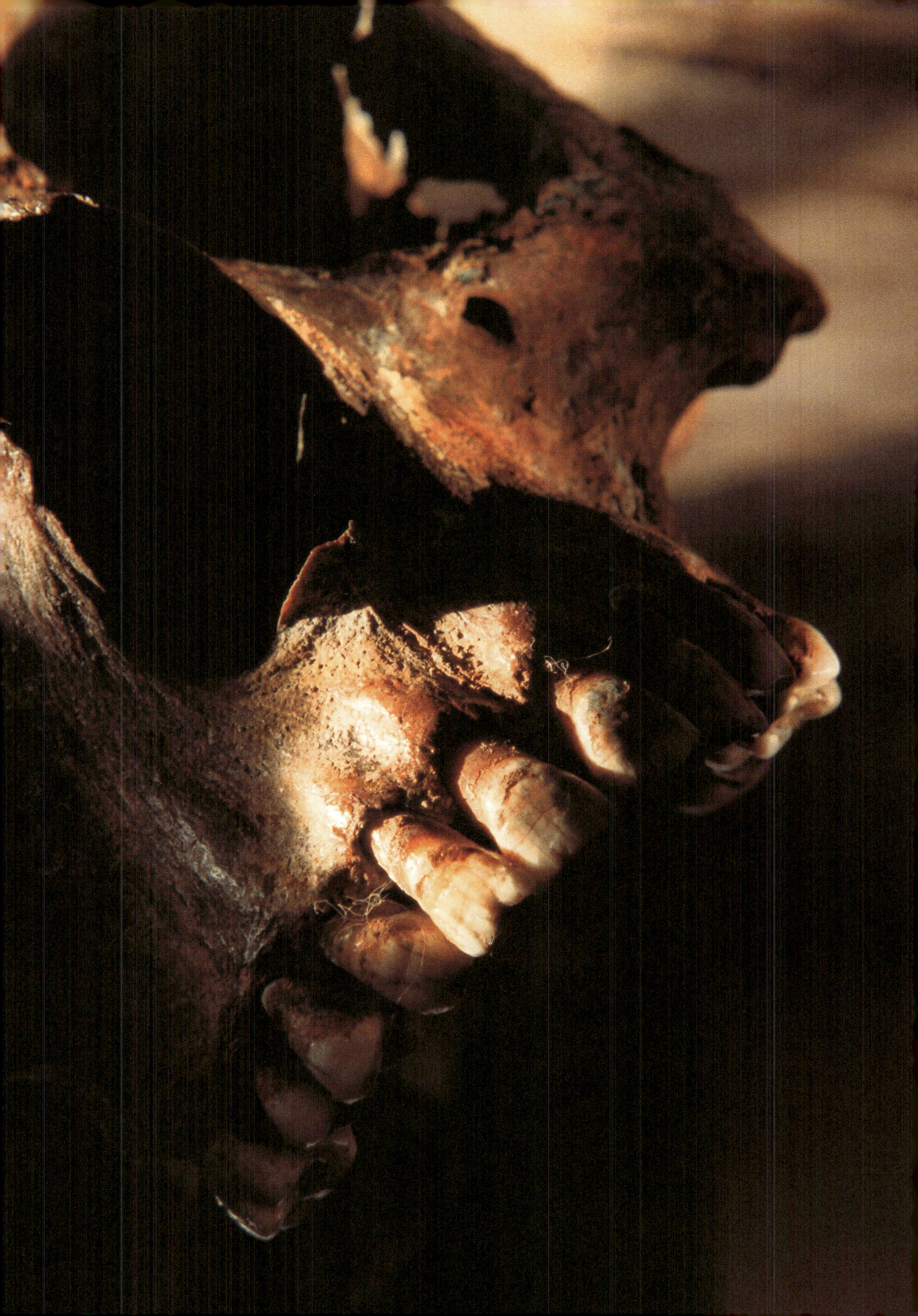

had escaped, letting out other prisoners into the bargain. While on the loose, he had not gone home to his wife but had hidden in the home of a certain Gertrud Matsdotter in Norrmalm. True to form, he had promised her marriage, "had irregular union" with her and made plans to move to another town.

But Thomas's real wife was an enterprising woman and Stockholm was a small town. She found out where her husband was hiding and told the police where he was and what he was up to. Thomas was arrested again. By now, the court was tired of the thieving whoremonger from The Black Dog. Thomas was sentenced to death.

His wench, Gertrud Matsdotter, was given the same sentence, for simple whoring, which meant sexual relations with a married person. Normal practice was for a higher court to reduce the death sentence to a forty *daler* fine. It was scarcely believable that Gertrud would be able to raise such a sum. She was certainly given the lash instead.

The skeletons of two women were found on the Vasa. Beata, the name given to this skull by the osteologists, was a little more than twenty when she died. The dark lines on her teeth meant that she had been undernourished as a child.

"Copper Matt" was the name given to the figure on top of the pillories by the scaffold in Stortorget, Main Square, in Stockholm.

Tobacco and Backgammon

HE PLAYED ON his Jew's harp and blew on his horn; cleverly he sang and was never forlorn. That was written about Olof Rudbeck, one of the most prominent figures of the 17th century in Sweden. When he sang, his rich bass easily drowned out twelve trumpets and four kettledrums.

Singing and playing musical instruments were important entertainments in the 17th century. Learning to sing and play the lute or another stringed instrument was part of an aristocrat's education. Among the sculptures on the Vasa are those of gods, emperors, heroes, warriors and lions, and also a little musical group. It is playing a folk dance tune at the entrance to the admiral's cabin. The line-up is bagpipes, lute, shawm (a primitive oboe), violin, viola and harp.

When Gustavus Adolphus was searching abroad for skilled professionals to accomplish the transformation of Sweden, he not only knocked on the doors of Dutch bankers, Flemish mining entrepreneurs and German gunsmiths but also of musicians. Andreas Düben, a German organist, was given a salary of three hun-

Gambling attracted the high-born and the low. The King once lost a hundred Hungarian "guldens" gambling at the house of Kasper the Apothecary. The treasurer's office settled the debt.

The lute has been signed by Vendelio Venere and was made in Padua around 1600. Notice the use of rib cravel, a style with a nautical touch.

Angels, kings and queens played the lute. This angel on the organ in Bälinge church, not far north of Stockholm, was carved by Mårten Redtmer.

Wind instruments had a shrill, piercing tone. The cornett is from the 16th century and is made of ivory. The shawm was fashioned from boxwood around 1680.

dred *daler* a year, as much as a naval officer. And 23 German musicians arrived in Stockholm at Midsummer in 1620, at the King's invitation. They made up the King's renowned Chamber Orchestra to the Royal Court and, according to one source, played wherever the opportunity arose: in church, at the court, at dinner, at sea and on land. Day and night.

Later, a French and an Italian chamber orchestra were to arrive. And whenever the King was at home between military campaigns, Queen Maria Eleonora could strum a lute for her hero.

Music was important at performances and at the theatre, as entertainment at the dinner table and for when the guests needed exercise after having partaken of a dinner. A polska dance in undulating three-quarter time, his grip firm on a maid-

The habit of tobacco smoking reached Sweden in the first decades of the 17th century. Seamen seem to have been heavy smokers and the practice was said to be beneficial for those of "moist nature". Onboard battleships, smoking was allowed only around the galley, according to a regulation dating from 1628. The reason was fire danger.

Several different games were found onboard the Vasa, among them this complete backgammon game. It had almost certainly been made by one of the officers on board.

The most common methods of conserving food were to salt or dry it. Islanders from the Stockholm archipelago supplied the city's citizens and the fleet's ships with salted Baltic herring in barrels and dried pike.

en's stout waist, set a man's blood coursing and his digestion to work on the small fowl, fattened capon, crayfish and sprat, fresh and smoked salmon, cucumber and a variety of mashes, jellied capers, olives, oysters, *medvurst* sausauge from Lübeck, flounder from Riga, smoked ham, almonds and marzipan, chestnuts, Seville oranges, confectioneries, fresh lemons and pastries.

The King himself was a skilful dancer and when there were too few young ladies, or they were too tired or too plain – as happened at a ball in Frankfurt in the early 1630s – new *Mädchen* were quickly recruited so that the ball could continue. When he, fired by the dance, "graciously caressed" a beautiful maiden called Anna Maria Bresler, she became so agitated that she tore his lace collar. It has been preserved, a souvenir of a passionate gentleman and his dancing skill.

But wilder scenes were played out. When Dutchman Abraham Kabeljo arranged a ball in Stockholm for his countrymen in the summer of 1628, it ended in a court case. The guests danced and shrieked until four in the morning. This was a serious matter, the court intoned, since it was the morning of Prayer Day, when the King had decreed all should be sober and penitent and go to church. No commerce was permitted on Prayer Days and no journeys undertaken except to church. The annual Prayer Days were an example of the links between material power and the church in the 17th century. On each of the four Prayer Days, priests would read from the pulpit the Prayer Day Bill, the King's letter to his people. These allowed him to argue for his policies, egg on his people or threaten them if the need arose. Abraham Kabeljo's guests were utterly indifferent. "What have your Prayer Days got to do with us?" one of the guests boldly answered the court. A classic example of culture clash between a nation and its immigrants, four hundred years ago.

Entertainments were many and intense in these years of armament. The capital was full of people with no real residential rights – not only foreigners but seamen, professional soldiers, craftsmen and merchants with no homes or families. When big military campaigns were being planned, soldiers and seamen were not allowed to return to their home districts. The reason was the fear of being without men to man the ships when they put to sea again in spring. It was, namely, not unusual for a third of them to disappear or not answer a summons when it was time to report for service.

The burghers of Stockholm were expected to provide room and board for military personnel and the other inhabitants had to pay an extra tax. They could manage "only with tears and great effort," in the words of a petition.

What was there to do for the seamen, soldiers and other temporary guests of the city? Card games were popular but were seen as being sinful and degraded. "I am suffering greatly on this fire," a card player moans in the ceiling painting of a church in Kinnarumma as hellfires scorch him.

Backgammon was less sinful. Expressions such as "five-two," "dozen-pair" and "rivets" were familiar to all, in all walks of life. This ancient game was extraordinarily popular in the 17th century and the round backgammon pieces often bore the King's image in relief. The King played backgammon as well. In 1625 he had a bad run. In a game at the house of Kasper the Apothecary, his majesty lost one hundred Hungarian *guldens*. This represented a fortune but, being a king, Gustavus Adolphus could withdraw the money from the treasurer's office. The receipt has been preserved.

The previous year, at a game of backgammon involving Simon Mickelsson and Johan Brun in a beer cellar, there was only 16 *öre* at stake. But the game ended with Johan stabbing Simon's head with his rapier. It went so deep, according to one of the city's guards, that the assailant had to tug twice "before he extracted the rapier from the skull." Simon died immediately and Johan was executed. When archaeologists flushed out the sludge from the Vasa's decks, they found an intact backgammon game towards the ship's stern. The light and dark tongues of the board were still visible and the pieces and dice were whole. The pieces were turned in ash and oak, the tongues cut from maple and pear wood. This beautiful game must have belonged to one of the officers.

The oldest evidence for another vice – if playing backgammon is indeed one – comes from the Vasa. In a barrel on the orlop deck, stored together with a cloth purse containing coins, some shoes, shoe pegs, a few wooden spoons and a small supply of food, lay a clay pipe.

The 17th century's Dutch masters loved painting burlesque scenes from inn life. The Netherlands was also the country most visited by Swedish students travelling abroad. The inn scenes painted by David Teniere were thus familiar to many Swedes.

Columbus's sailors brought tobacco plants to Europe and they spread quickly across the continent. As early as in 1518, tobacco was being grown in Spain and Portugal for medicinal purposes as well as for decoration. The secretary of King Henri II of France, Jean Nicot de Villemain, travelled to Portugal as ambassador in the mid-1500s. In 1550, he sent some of "this divine medicament" to France. He claimed it would cure headaches and make people more relaxed. The names of the plant in Latin, *Nicotiana tobacum*, as well as the drug nicotine are in memory of the ambassador.

Sailors and soldiers spread the habit of, as it was originally called in Swedish, "drinking tobacco." In 1628, the Admiral of the Realm drew up regulations for smoking on board naval vessels. "Shall also be prohibited to either drink or use tobacco anywhere on board with the exception of the galley," said the sea articles of that year. Sweden's first academic treatise on tobacco was published in 1633. The author was Johannes Franck, a professor of anatomy and botany at Uppsala University, and his dissertation described the blessings and dangers of tobacco.

Smoking is beneficial for those of "damp disposition" and for the elderly, noted the professor. He recommended smoking for fishermen and sailors and others who lived by the water. It was, nevertheless, harmful for choleric people and those angry by nature and with "dry temperaments, since it infects the head, causes dizziness and provokes headaches".

Singers should smoke, wrote the professor, since smoke makes the voice strong, clear and pleasing. Olof Rudbeck, the man whose voice could overpower twelve trumpets and four kettledrums, must have been a heavy smoker.

THE SAGA OF THE VASA

The warship Vasa was incomparable. Incomparably beautiful with its decor of sculptures. Incomparably useless as a ship. Incomparably exciting as a time machine.

The Right Stuff

FROM HER WINDOW, Dame Brita of Ängsö by Lake Mälaren could see the long line of sleds snaking over the inlet's ice. In the winter of 1625, she had sold oaks to the two Dutchmen, the Hybertsson brothers, at the shipyard in Stockholm. Payment was 1,152 *daler* and 16 *öre*, according to the contract she drew up. A standing oak cost two and a half *daler* said another contract drawn up by the Hybertsson brothers the same year. Almost five hundred oak trees would be felled on Dame Brita's property during that winter of 1625.

Oak was best for building ships. Oaks were thus reserved for the navy's needs and were not to be felled without royal permission. Oak was also a valuable trade commodity in the 17th century. Norway especially exported large quantities of oak timber to Holland. Every part of the tree was put to use.

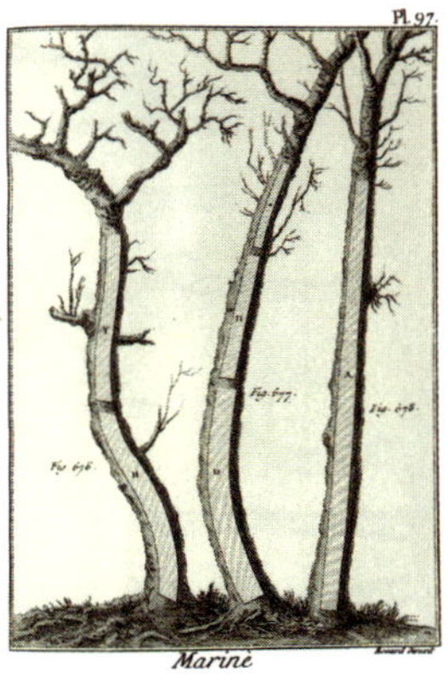

A portrait exists of her, painted at that time. It can be seen halfway up the stairs in Ängsö manor, beside the bird-plucking room and the hare room. Dame Brita is dressed in a light grey, pleated mourning dress. Her gaze is sombre and determined and she looks straight back at her observer. Her eyelids are heavy, her eyebrows highly arched and her mouth firmly shut. She was one of so many women who looked after hearth and home while their husbands were away – at war, on a mission for the King or gone for good. At the time, a third of all the farms in Sweden were run by women.

Dame Brita had her hands full. Her property comprised two hundred farms and crofts in eight provinces. In addition, she was Hand and Neck Adjudicator, with the right to sentence wrong-doings, even as far as to administering the death penalty. This was a unique aristocratic right which survived in parts of Sweden until the end of the 17th century. The widow of Ängsö, Dame Brita, was a steadfast woman. The manor chapel still has the veil she dropped when the spirit of her dead husband visited her during a dawn Christmas service in the 1620s.

As long as warships were built of wood, oak remained hard currency. A law enacted on 4 August 1608 made it a punishable offence to cut down an oak tree without proper permission. The first offence brought a fine of ten *daler*. The second, twenty. The third offence was punishable by death.

This winter, Ängsö was invaded by carpenters, woodcutters, smiths and about forty seamen. They had templates to help them select the right timber. With them, they brought axes, saws, hoists, jacks, grindstones and more.

Every ship needed special timber. The size of the ship determined which trees the master builder chose. Branches and crooked trunks were carefully measured against the templates and given uses. They were made into strong ribs, bottom timbers and knees with the wood fibres following the ship's lines.

Felling five hundred sturdy oaks was a tough job. Dragging the thick trunks and crooked branches down to the lake's ice was even harder. After the spring thaw,

A portrait of Dame Brita Bååt hangs in Ängsö manor. Dame Brita ran the manor and its business and in 1625 signed a contract for the delivery of five hundred oaks to the builders of the Vasa.

the seamen had the job of floating, pulling, rowing, sailing and towing the cargo to Stockholm. Transporting the timber cost almost as much the timber itself.

Keeping tight control over income and expenses was vital. In 1625, there had been a re-organisation at the Swedish navy's most important shipyard, Skeppsgården in Stockholm. Operations had, to use a modern term, been privatised. The sub-contractors were the Hybertsson brothers, and the Ängsö timber order was the biggest they had negotiated. They would need a large supply of timber for several years. According to a contract signed in 1625, they were to build two large warships and two smaller ships in the next four years. One of these was to be the Vasa. The brothers were also contracted to provide maintenance and repairs for the warships moored in Stockholm. Payment was an incredible 66,000 *daler* a year. As it turned out, the sum was inadequate. And moreover, the King turned out to be a grudging debtor. Payments were irregular and when there was no money in the treasury, they were not made at all.

The two brothers had a gigantic task. Purchase of nails alone came to 2,960 *daler* - a year's pay for a hundred seamen. On top of that came sawn timber, tar, tallow, grease, candles, paint, glue and glass. There was seal oil for the lamps, cow hide for the pumps and animal hair for caulking. There were saw blades, iron pots, anchors, reed and much more.

Arndt Hybertsson, also known as de Groot the Great was in charge of purchasing. He travelled to the most disparate countries to find what he needed; he bought compasses in Holland, sawn oak planks in Königsberg, Germany, seal blubber in Åland (between Sweden and Finland), saw blades and iron pots in west-central Sweden and tar in Hälsingland province. He ordered his cast block-sheaves from Nikolaus the Caster and tallow candles from the wife of Lembrigt Candlemaker. Orphans, criminals and the residents of the Riddarholmen poorhouse in Stockholm spun thread, painted and sewed to his orders. De Groot even brewed beer for his own consumption and for the other immigrant sub-contractors since Swedish small beer was not good enough for Dutch palates.

The Skeppsgården shipyard was, at the time, Stockholm's biggest employer by far. In this time of war, the Swedish capital was little more than arms producer, storehouse, shipyard and harbour for the Swedish fleet. Stockholm was a small town, with a little more than 10,000 inhabitants, most of whom were involved in one way or another with the Skeppsgården construction work. There were carpenters, woodcutters, smiths, borers, caulkers, coopers, riveters, platform-makers, mast-builders, block-makers, wood-carvers, sail-makers, rope-makers and hemp-spinners who all bought fish, sea-birds eggs and seal meat from the archipelago

Oaks destined for ship construction should be felled in winter. Winter timber contains less sap. Several centuries-old oaks still grow at Ängsö manor on the northern bank of Lake Mälaren, near Stockholm. They were still saplings when trees were felled here for the Vasa.

The signature of Dutch businessman Arndt De Groot. He and his brother, Master Henrik, built the Vasa. (next pages)

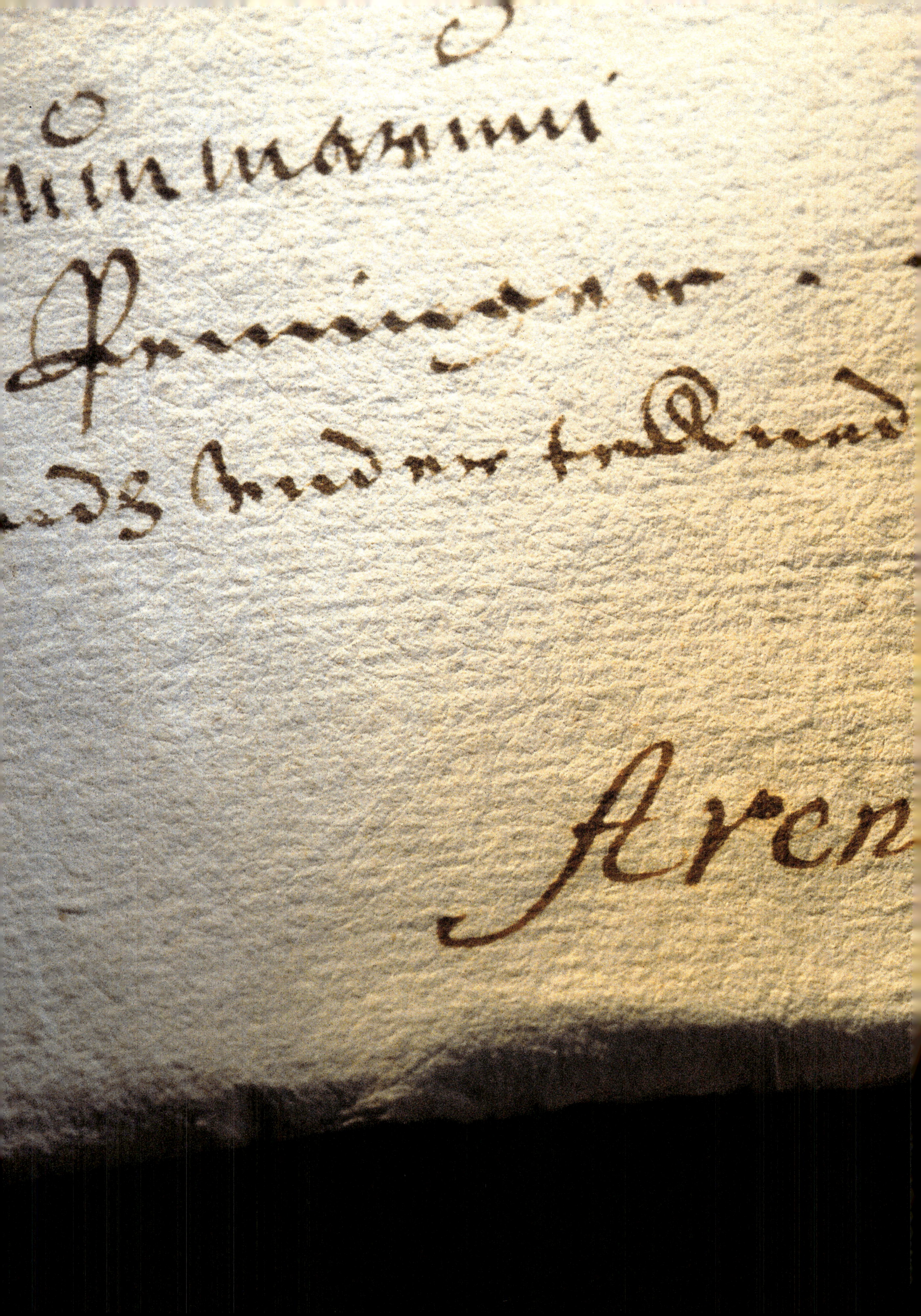
Aren

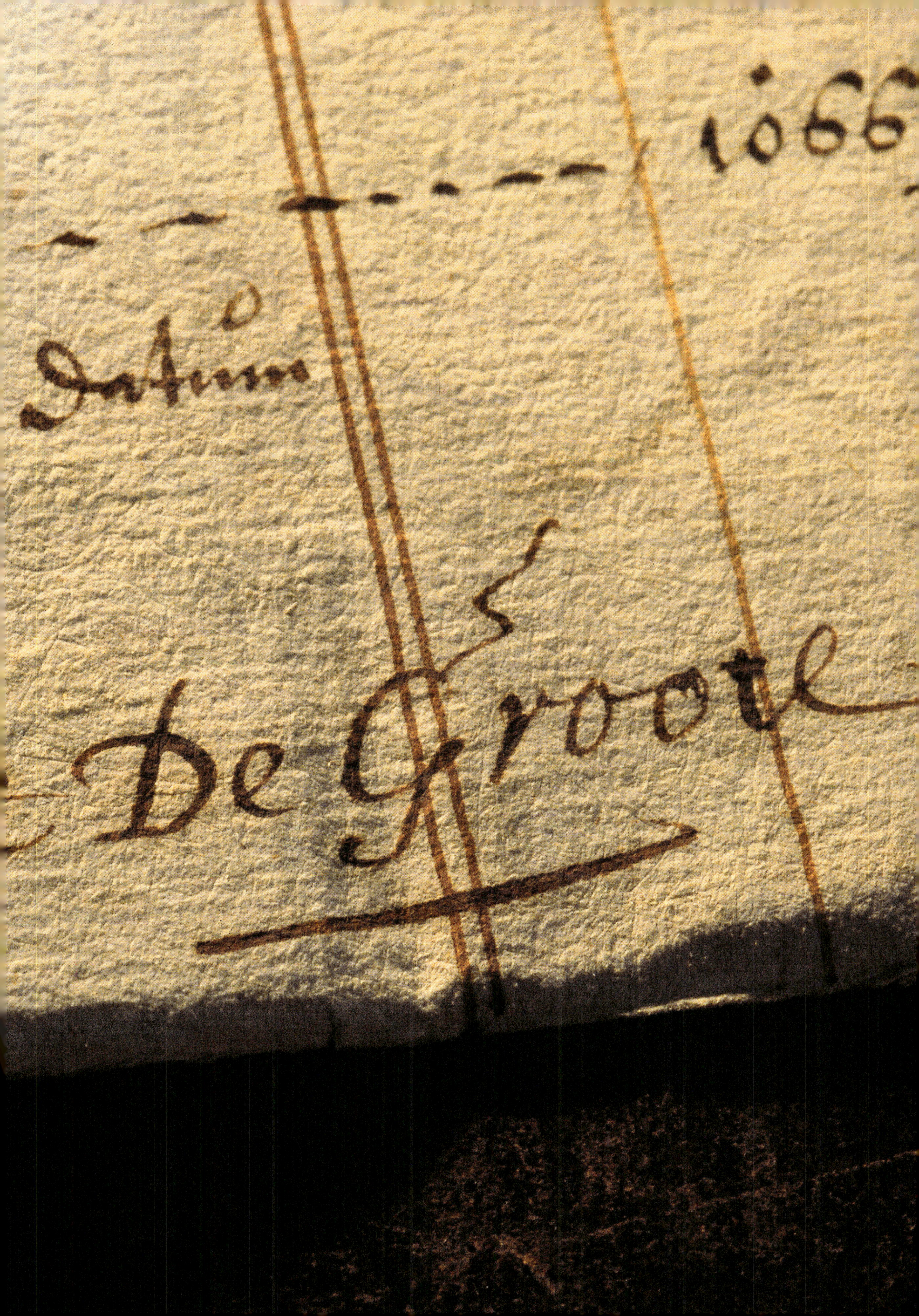
1666
Datum
De Groote

traders who supplied the capital city with most of its perishable commodities.

The shipyard's sawyers brawled in the inns and the seamen paid surreptitious visits to Margareta the Cod, Karin Clubfoot and Fat Sara to be duly punished by the lash on the city's main square.

One of the worst marine disasters in Swedish history occurred in the autumn of 1625. In mid-September, a large part of the Swedish fleet was lost in the Gulf of Riga. A Swedish naval squadron ran into a storm and ten ships were driven into shallow water and stranded.

The disaster in Riga Bay had an immediate effect on the construction projects at Skeppsgården shipyard and put extra pressure on the Hybertsson brothers. The King was anxious to take delivery of his ships on schedule.

Late in the winter of 1626, building of the Vasa began, with the launch of its hull as early as the summer of that year. But the ship was far from complete.

There were no blueprints or even calculations for the construction. The builders used their experience and a set of key figures which allowed them to plot the ship's measurements at different parts of the hull. These included the length, the angles and the arcs. The measurements had been approved by the King.

Master builder Henrik and his trusted shipbuilder Hein Jakobsson, however, did not appear to be completely satisfied with the measurements. This was revealed at the hearing which followed the ship's sinking. "I worked with the measurements I was given by Master Henrik and which the King had ordered," Hein Jakobsson claimed in his defence, when accused by the prosecution of building a

There were no construction blueprints in the 17th century. Master shipbuilders made their calculations from the relationship between given measurements, circles and arcs.

The main naval shipyard in Stockholm glimpsed from one of the eastern windows of Three Crowns Palace. The year is 1634 and there is a thick forest of masts. The view is a detail from a portrait of the youthful Queen Kristina.

worthless vessel. Hein went on: "but I even added an extra foot and five thumbs to the width. And everyone said it was well built." A foot and five thumbs is about a half-metre.

The gunports on the Vasa and the windows of the Royal Bakery in Stockholm. A large part of the capital's population was occupied in building and equipping the naval fleet. The Royal Bakery delivered ship's biscuits and bread to the army and navy.

Many of the Swedish fleet's ships ran aground in the shallow waters near Domesnäs at the mouth of the Bay of Riga in the autumn of 1625. (next pages)

Only a few months after construction of the Vasa began, the Skeppsgården shipyard received payment. On 22 July, 1626, Master Henrik complained that the Crown still owed him nineteen thousand *daler*. He had to wait until 31 August for an answer: he could have three thousand *daler*, but not until a few weeks later. The Swedish state finances were at rock bottom, and it did not help much that Chancellor Axel Oxenstierna went with cap in hand to prominent nobles to raise money for ships to replace those lost in the Gulf of Riga. Oxenstierna himself donated two thousand *daler*, with an equal amount coming from Jakob De la Gardie. How much was ultimately collected is unclear but it was insufficient for even one large ship. The cost of the Vasa was estimated at forty thousand *daler*. Arndt de Groot had his own way of tackling the lack of money – by smuggling oak timber to Holland.

On 16 January 1628, the King himself visited the shipyard. Master Henrik had died and it may have been his widow Margareta who received the King and showed him the ship. We have no way of knowing whether he was satisfied or not. In any event, he was displeased later that year; the ship was not being completed fast enough. During the summer, two councillors were charged with week-

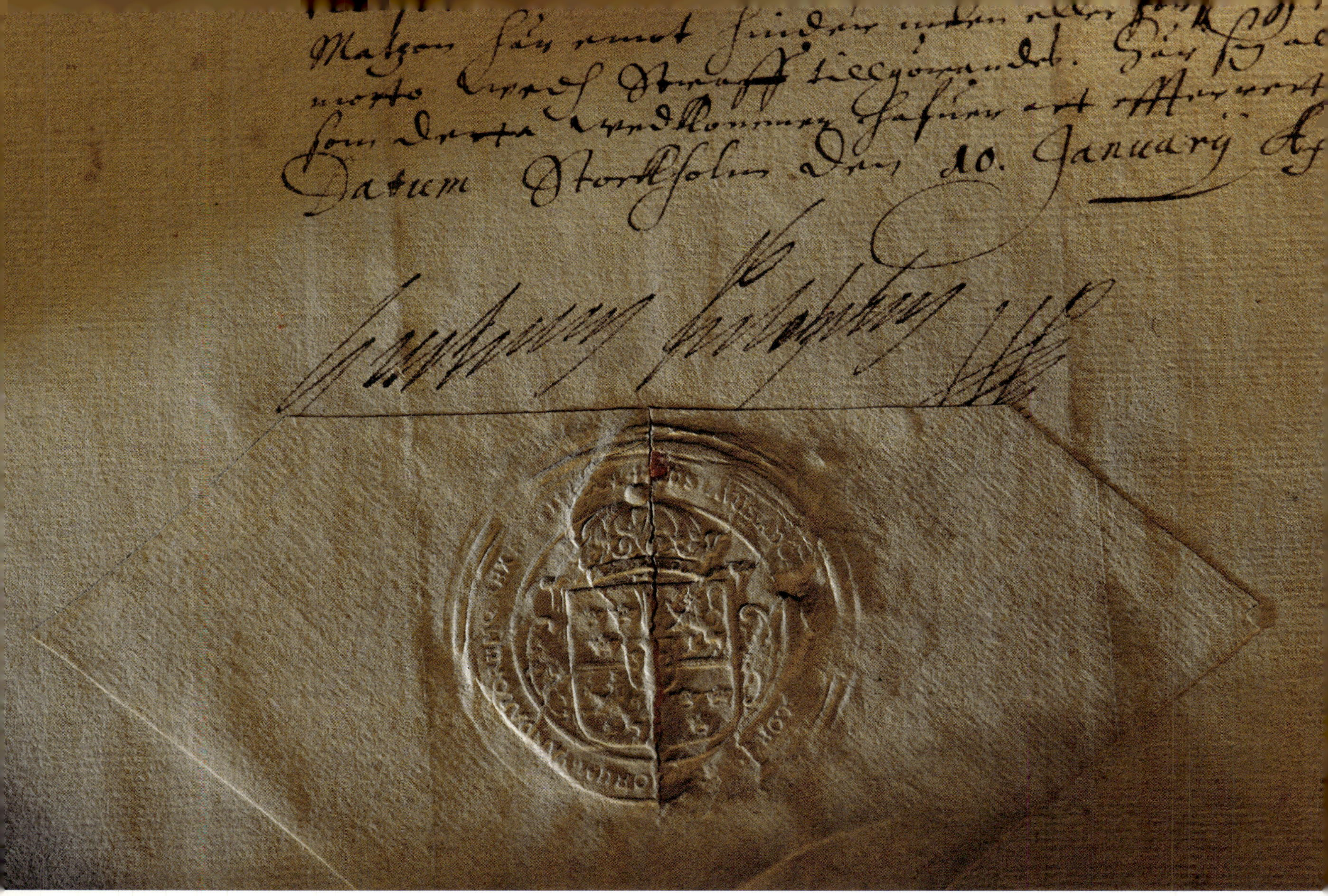
Datum Stockholm den 10. January

The signature and seal of Gustavus Adolphus. During the inquest into the sinking of the Vasa, the shipbuilders claimed that the ship's dimensions had been approved by the King himself.

ly inspections of the construction and on 22 June, the King demanded in a letter that the Vasa should be finished by, at the latest, "next Jacob's Day," which meant by 25 July. At that time, the Vasa was moored by the Three Crowns castle. There, 64 cannon were taken on board, along with ammunition and other equipment. A difficult task was the loading of ballast. In this case, the ballast was 120 tonnes of round stones which had to be placed, one by one, in the dark and narrow hold.

At this stage, everyone concerned must have seen that catastrophe was imminent. The Vasa was unstable – too unstable.

The Vasa was a large ship for its day but not so large that an experienced seaman must have sensed something wrong as soon as he put his foot onboard. And there were many experienced seamen involved: first and foremost, Söfring Hansson, who was to captain the Vasa on its maiden voyage. Söfring had been an active seaman since the end of the previous century, when he deserted from a Danish ship to enlist on the Swedish side. In 1602, he was the commander of a Swedish ship, the Blå Falken; in 1609 commander of the Riddare Sankt Göran and others after that. He must have noticed that something was amiss on the

Vasa. Another experienced sailor, Hans Jonsson, was also involved. He was a pilot who had grown up in the Stockholm archipelago and who had commanded ships since the beginning of the 1600s.

But others must also have seen that the King's new ship did not move as it should; they must have felt it in their seamen's legs and bodies. Quartermaster Göran Matsson, for example, must have noticed, and Chief Boatswain Per Bertilsson as well as the master shipbuilder himself, Hein Jakobsson.

Why was nothing done? In fact, something was done. Söfring Hansson approached one of the navy's top men, Vice-Admiral Clas Fleming. Fleming, in contrast to Hansson, was not a real seaman. Looking back at Sweden's swift transformation in the early 17th century, researchers often point out that officials were most often appointed for their capability rather than rank or birth. Unfortunately, this was not always the case in the navy.

Originally a captain in the cavalry, Fleming became a confidant of the King and was appointed vice-admiral in 1620, though lacking in real seafaring experience. However, in the years up to 1628, Clas Fleming spent a lot of time at sea, though with some lack of success – in that time, he lost several ships under his command. But he must have known something was wrong. Admiral Fleming and Captain Söfring Hansson ordered thirty men to run back and forth across the deck of the Vasa. But when they had made three runs, they were ordered to stop: the Vasa was threatening to capsize at quayside! The ballast was checked once again, but it was deemed impossible to fit more in. "I went down with a light and a lantern myself to inspect," said Quartermaster Matsson later.

The coat of arms of the Ekstubbe (Oak Stump) family, from the 1630s. Whoever felled an oak without permission suffered a heavy fine. A repeat offence was punishable by death.

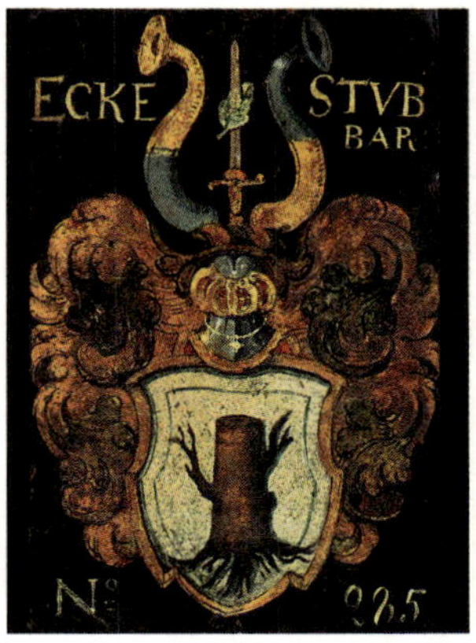

The Vasa was too special. It was a few decimetres too narrow below the waterline, the keel too heavily reinforced, the sculptures too large and, especially, the cannon too many. But this was the King's expressed wish; even as a child, he had had a weakness for ships bristling with guns.

When he was five, he had seen the Swedish fleet in Kalmar harbour. Someone asked the young royal which ship he found most pleasing. He pointed out the Svarte Ryttaren: "That one, because it has most cannon!" The Vasa had 48 thick, heavy 24-pounder cannon weighing 1,300 kilograms each, and 16 smaller cannon.

"If only His Majesty were at home," exclaimed Admiral Fleming when he stopped the stability test. But the King was in Prussia and the Vasa set sail. There was very little wind. It was Sunday, 10 August, 1628 - a bad luck day, according to folklore.

AΩ
SOLI DEO GLORIA
CALENDARIUM PERPETUUM
MENSIS
AVGVST.
DIES
XXXI
ORIENS
ORTUS SOLIS
OCCASUS SOLIS
OCCIDENS
Longitudo Diei
Hora
Longitudo Noctis
V
VII
CURSUS SOLIS IN
DIES
Festorum
Sanctorum
Catenæ Petri
Transfigur. Chr.
Laurentius
Ascensio M. in Cœl.
Bernhardus
Bartholomaeus
7. 8. 9. 10. 11. 12. 13.
Dies SOLIS
Dies LUNÆ
Dies MARTIS
Dies MERCURI
Dies IOVIS
Dies VENERIS
Dies SATURNI

Unhappy Overture

IN STOCKHOLM ON Sunday 10 August 1628, the wind had finally died to a breeze. The change was welcome; the summer had been windy and rainier than in human memory – so wet that even King Gustavus Adolphus complained about the weather in a letter. As so often during these years, he was in Elbing on Poland's Baltic coast. He wrote that his barber-surgeon had been washed into the sea, wagon and all, because of the flooding. It was perhaps the kind of exaggeration those who complain about the weather are prone to, but there were many complainers that summer of 1628. The soldiers at the siege of Stralsund looked like drowned cats in their trenches, observed an eyewitness.

But now, in early August, the skies cleared and the winds died. Chancellor Axel Oxenstierna boarded a ship at Baltiysk, the Swedish base on the Gulf of Danzig, to sail to the site of the siege. The journey should have taken three days on the open sea but took an entire week. "A delightful dry period for the farmers but feeble breezes for the sailor," the chancellor commented.

The tenth of August was a recognised bad-luck day. This Calendarium perpetuum or adjustable calendar was used at the beginning of the 17th century and shows dates and astrological movements. The Vasa sank on 10 August 1632.

In Stockholm, too, they were waiting for feeble breezes. The new ship Vasa was tied up, fully equipped, just below the royal palace. It had probably been moored there for several days or even a week, awaiting suitable weather.

From now on, the saga of the Vasa became like a Greek tragedy staged by Sophocles or one of the other classic tragedians. Those involved anticipate what is to happen but cannot do anything to stop it. What propels events is the King's wish to take delivery of his new ship. The crew of the Vasa can only play their predestined roles. Events unfold but fate cannot be avoided. The Vasa is in God's hands. Those on board who expect the worst put their trust in God and his providence. "I die when God wishes it," said Gustavus Adolphus once, when warned against placing himself in the first line of battle. That same religious fatalism permeated the time and the crew of the Vasa almost certainly shared it.

There are no exact records but there were perhaps 150 crew and military personnel on board and a number of guests. One of the latter was Hans Jonsson, known as "the Old Captain." There were also a number of women: wives, sweethearts and children of the crew. They had been given permission to accompany their menfolk on the first part of the trip but were to disembark at Vaxholm, the last large community in the archipelago before the open sea.

Between three and four o'clock on the afternoon of 10 August, the Vasa finally cast off from its mooring place below Three Crowns castle. For several reasons, it was an extraordinary day and an extraordinary time of day.

Firstly, it was a Sunday, and sea voyages seldom begin on Sundays. The only voyages not frowned on are those that go to and from church. Also the date was known to be an unlucky one and few dared challenge bad-luck omens in the 17th century. It was very late in the day if the objective was to get the women and children to Vaxholm before dark. On 10 August in a leap year such as 1628, the sun went down in Stockholm at 19 minutes past seven. After which darkness falls rapidly. (At the time, the old Julian calendar was still in use in Sweden; according to our current calendar, the Vasa sank on 21 August.) There was no way that a ship like the Vasa could sail through the tricky archipelago waters in dusk and darkness. With the light following wind that was blowing, the ship could scarcely make more than ten nautical miles before dusk. Vaxholm would still be in the distance.

The reason the Vasa left so late was probably that Captain Söfring Hansson was gravely worried about the ship's stability and realised that it could not handle more than an extremely light wind. In that case, late afternoon is a logical time to set sail. In a summer of low pressure like that of 1628, the water temperature is low and morning breezes are often fresh southwesterlies – too fresh for the Vasa. At midday, the wind changes to an easterly sea breeze, an impossible wind for a ship sailing due east from Stockholm and which cannot tack in the archipelago's narrow channels. What remained was the soft wind that follows the sea breeze in late afternoon. Which was when the Vasa set off.

The fateful voyage began by Three Crowns castle. The wind was a gentle southwesterly and for the first hundred metres, the seamen kedged the ship forward, dragging it by the anchor. Then, where the large locks are today between the Old Town and Södermalm district, the course became more easterly and the captain set the sails. Even though the wind was weak, the captain hoisted only four of the ten sails the Vasa was built to carry. In fact, he wanted even fewer sails unfurled. At the hearing later, he said: "We set the topsail only because we were afraid of hitting the shore." He must have been extraordinarily concerned.

The Vasa moved slowly, slowly forward leeward of the high cliffs of Södermalm. The first thousand metres took almost an hour. Then, where the cliff-face ends and before a new cliff appears at a place now called Fåfängan, the Vasa left its lee. There was a slight gust of wind, which was all it took. The ship heeled over to port, righted itself, but with the next gust, keeled over on its side, its sails and rigging dipping into the water and water rushing in. The King's new ship sank immediately.

The wind had been so weak that the lines did not run out through the blocks, "even though they were newly greased," as Lieutenant Gjerdsson later told the shipwreck hearing. Modern shipbuilders have assessed the Vasa's stability and calculated that it would have keeled over in a wind of four metres per second – an extremely gentle breeze. In a letter to the King, the council of the realm described the events in detail: "When the ship advanced to the inlet at Tegelvik bay, more weather filled the sails, and shortly there began a considerable heeling leeward, though she corrected herself in the water, when, close on Beckholm island, she fell to her side, with water entering the gun ports until she slowly sank with sails aloft, flags flying and all."

"Slowly," wrote the council. But much indicates that the accident happened quickly. At the hearing, squadron commander Vice-Admiral Erik Jönsson Krämer

The helmsman's post on the Vasa. This vertical pole, the whipstaff, steered the ship. The steering compartment was below deck and the helmsman had no forward visibility at all. He steered to orders from an officer on deck.

The stern part of the Vasa's upper deck. (next pages)

recounted that he had rushed down to the gun deck when the ship started heeling. He had wanted to check that the cannon were properly fastened to their mountings. The admiral's sense of duty almost cost him his life. When he got below deck, the water was already so high that ladders and stairs had loosened and floated adrift. With extreme difficulty, he made his way back to the main deck and safety.

But rushing from the stern, where the admiral had been stationed, across the main deck, down a ladder to the gun deck and back up again, would take no more than thirty seconds. It cannot have taken much longer before the Vasa sank.

The number of bodies found in the Vasa when it was salvaged in 1961 also indicates that it happened quickly. Most of the crew must have been on the main deck when the accident happened. The ship had just set sail and many crew members were needed on deck to clear up after the sails had been set and to look after the sails that were up. Large warships of this kind were very hard to manoeuvre in narrow channels. They were steered partly by their sails, which demanded knowledge, close attention and many people on deck and in the rigging.

Abraham Brahe wrote in his diary on 10 August 1628: "Between four o'clock and five, the great, new ship Vasa keeled over and sank."

Those on deck must have had a decent chance of survival, even if few could swim. The Vasa's masts were sticking out of the water after the ship keeled over, giving the crew something to hold onto. Planks and loose pieces of wood were

certainly floating in the water, to be used as flotation help. And "many boats were soon there," as an eyewitness wrote.

When the Vasa was salvaged, the remains of at least sixteen people were found inside. They must have been shut in when the ship went down. There were at least three possible escape routes: to the fore, midships and to the stern. If the Vasa keeled over and sank slowly, even the most duty-conscious seaman would have had time to rush from his post to safety.

Besides, five skeletons were found on the Vasa's starboard side, that is, on the windward side. This indicates that the poor souls rushed to starboard when the ship began heeling to port. Or were they washed starboard by the in-rushing water? In any event, the Vasa was filled with water before they could get out and they drowned in the cramped gun decks.

Parts of the Vasa's thick anchor cable have been saved after 350 years on the seabed.

The Vasa sailed only about a thousand metres before it keeled over. This model of the ship is on a scale of 1:10. (next pages)

What were these people doing below decks? The Vasa had fired a salute on leaving the inner harbour. Perhaps men were on the gun decks clearing up after the salvoes. The ship had also been dragged forward using anchors for the very first part of the journey. The lines used for the manoeuvre would have to be stowed and the capstan on the lower gun deck would have to be looked after. Perhaps the victims were occupied with these chores. We do not know exactly how many died in the accident since the crew lists were lost. There are, however, three sources to turn to. The first is a letter from Gabriel Gustafsson Oxenstierna, the brother of Chancellor Axel Oxenstierna. In the letter, the number of killed is estimated at "some thirty persons with seamen, women and children." Gabriel Gustafsson Oxenstierna also names one of the deceased, old Captain Hans Jonsson. He is the only one known to us by name.

The second source is a report sent home by Danish emissiary, Erik Krabbe. He estimated the number killed at "about fifty persons, among them several women and children." The third source is the English ambassador, James Spens. He makes the number about forty.

Estimates thus vary between thirty and more than fifty killed. If the reliability of the sources is to be compared, it can be noted that Oxenstierna had little cause to exaggerate the extent of the disaster - quite the contrary. His letter was also dated more than a week after the sinking and the number of dead would by then have been established.

Spens and especially Krabbe would have had nothing to lose by putting the figure as high as possible. In Denmark, a Swedish naval disaster would provoke little sorrow. Sweden and Denmark were in fact allies in this period, but there was much mutual distrust.

The Vasa's newly cast bronze cannon were stored in the old Three Crowns palace. In the summer of 1628, the ship was moored below the palace and the cannon and ballast were brought onboard. A stability test was ordered but was aborted when the Vasa almost tipped over at the quayside.

The number of drowned in the Vasa disaster must therefore have been thirty or more, but hardly as many as forty or fifty.

The remains of twenty-five people found by archaeologists in and around the Vasa must have been most of them.

Immediately after the accident, Captain Söfring Hansson was placed under arrest and those in positions of responsibility were debriefed.

"No one was drunk," said chief bosun Per Bertilsson. "The ship was built according to the specifications I was given," said master shipbuilder Hein Jakobsson. "All cannon were properly fastened," said Chief Ordnance Master Erik Krämer. "Apart from that, there is not much I know about ships," he added prudently. When the person ultimately responsible, the licensee of the shipyard, Arndt Hybertsson De Groot, was asked how he could built such a wretched ship, he answered: "The ship was faultlessly built, as everyone can testify." Besides, he defended himself, the King had approved of the length and breadth and "it pleased His Majesty". The ship was certainly well built, noted the chief interrogator sourly, but it did not have the right proportions. This concluded the hearing.

There was no further hearing and neither admiral, captain nor shipbuilder was punished. The fateful experiment in privatising the shipyard and licensing ship construction was ended that autumn.

In November, Arndt Hybertsson De Groot quietly left Sweden. If the Vasa disaster was the reason is unknown. He may have been nervous that financial irregularities would come to light since the Council had confiscated the shipyard's bookkeeping for 1627 and 1628. False auditing and embezzlement were not uncommon in Sweden in this time of expansion. The sermon preached to the Vasa crew before the ship left the dock had been selected by coincidence from The Gospel according to St. Luke, Chapter 16, Verses 1 to 9. It was about the unjust Dishonest Manager who was discovered embezzling his master.

Who, then, was responsible for the shipwreck of the Vasa? Marine historian Björn Landström, in his own book on the Vasa contends that the King himself was responsible since he laid down guidelines for construction and decided on the ship's weaponry and decoration.

Gustavus Adolphus was in Baltiysk on the other side of the Baltic when the Vasa went down. He first heard of the disaster on 27 August, more than two weeks afterwards. Hot-headed as he was, it was lucky for those involved that the King was far from Stockholm. "Imprudence and carelessness," was his spontaneous comment. He assumed that the gun ports had not been properly closed.

A few days later, on 8 September, the King wrote to Chancellor Axel Oxenstierna. It was a depressing letter. First, the King wrote that the Vasa had sunk. Besides, he wrote, the news had just come that Admiral Clas Fleming on his flagship, the Kristina, had gone aground on the German coast and that the ship had been set on fire by the enemy. Several other ships in the same squadron had been damaged in heavy weather and their crews "devastated" by illnesses. Therefore, wrote the King, "We graciously ask you" to inform the Danish king that Sweden could not help him with any ships that autumn.

Unfortunately, that was not all. The King did not yet know that his fleet had suffered yet another severe loss that unhappy summer of 1628. On 6 September, two days before he sat down to write to Oxenstierna, another of the King's vital warships had run aground and sunk. It was the Riksnyckeln, which went down in the south part of Stockholm's archipelago.

Men Who Walked Under the Water

LOOKING OUT FROM the eastern tower of Three Crowns castle on Sunday morning, 11 August 1628, you could clearly see three stumps sticking out of the water – the Vasa's three masts. The upper part of the topsail hung limply from its yards. The lower part was under the water's surface. Flags and the long pennants flapped in the morning breeze. But nothing could be seen of the ship itself. It lay thirty metres deep, with all its equipment and all the valuable cannon.

Quick action was typical for the time. And English engineer Ian Bulmer was a man of action. We do not know why he was in Stockholm in mid-August, 1628, although the city was thick with foreigners selling their services.

Two days after the accident, Bulmer sought an audience with the councillors of the realm, saying he knew how to salvage the ship. The very same day, the council sent a letter to the King telling him they had charged the "Englander" with raising the Vasa. In order not to irk the King - losing the Vasa was enough – they assured him that no money would be paid in advance.

Within a week, Bulmer had made good progress. Using hawsers, grapnels and "a variety of other instruments," he had brought the ship into an upright position. This in itself was a feat for which he was paid, with the King's approval, one thousand *daler*. This was a large sum of money. But then little more happened and Bulmer could salvage neither ship nor cannon.

Using a primitive diving bell, the "men who could walk underwater" were able to salvage most of the Vasa's valuable bronze cannon. This feat was performed more than thirty years after the shipwreck. Divers were able to work underwater for as long as thirty minutes.

Dangerous experiments were carried out to see if divers could extend their underwater working period. Air hoses and barrels of extra air were used. Anders the Diver coughed up blood for a week after one of these trials.

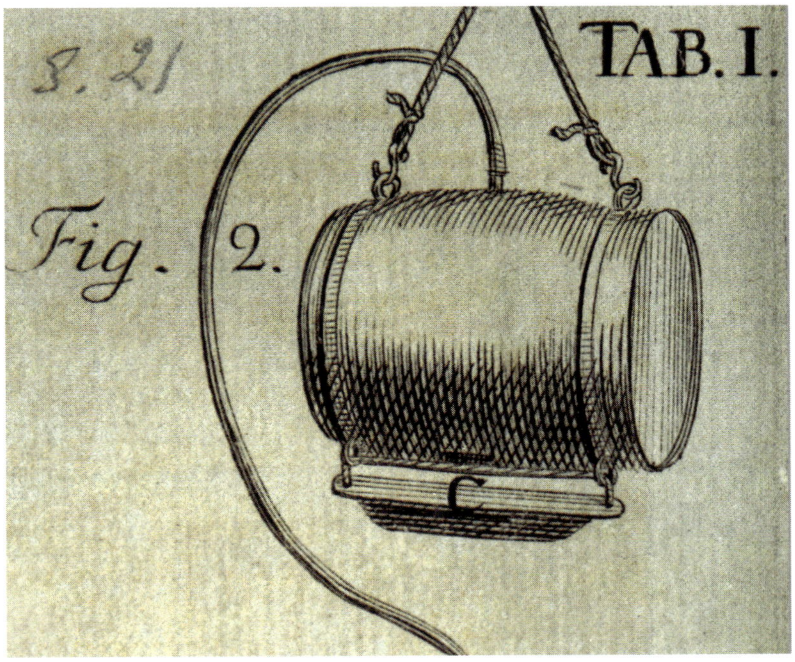

In the autumn, Vice-Admiral Clas Fleming and the Vasa's captain, Söfring Hansson, joined the salvage efforts on the orders of the King. In a letter dated 27 November, Fleming told the King that he trusted, after God, in Dutchmen if a salvage were to succeed. In January, he had given up on the Dutch and had begun to look for "men who could walk under water." He turned to the Swedish governor of Karelia, in eastern Finland, for help in finding divers. Why Fleming looked to Karelia for help is a mystery. Or is it?

Salvage divers have always been wild and rugged individuals. It may have been the reputation of Karelians for courage and resilience that prompted the councillors to start their search there. The bait was a decent wage, new tools and schnapps paid for by the King. Sure enough, in the spring a man called Long Hans disembarked in the Swedish capital accompanied by four Karelian divers. But Long Hans was to be just as unsuccessful as Bulmer in raising the Vasa.

The Vasa was carrying a total of 64 cannon when it sank. Of those, 48 were heavy 24-pounders in bronze. The 17th-century salvage divers did their work well; when the Vasa was lifted in 1961, only three were left.

For the next few decades, salvage divers and adventurers arrived in Stockholm from all of Europe, all of them captivated by the King's ship and its valuable cannon. Only two enjoyed some success: Hans Albrecht von Treileben from Värmland province and a German, Andreas Peckel. The two were partners, and headed a team of divers from all over Sweden.

The team made its dives in the 1660s. They used a diving bell much like a church bell in appearance. Their method was simple: the divers kept their heads and upper bodies inside the bell, breathing the compressed air. They were supported by a little platform under the bell.

The first diver brave enough to make the descent to the ship, thirty metres down, was Diver Anders, from the town of Vadstena in south central Sweden. "It looks like a poorly thrown together paling fence down there," he said. With pliers, poles and saws, they broke through the Vasa's deck, opened shut cannon port doors, detached the cannon from their mountings, wound hawsers around the guns and hoisted the heavy pieces to the surface. It sounds simple, but it was an incomparable feat by incomparable men.

There is an eyewitness account from 1663. The writer was an adventurous Italian priest, Francesco Negri. He was in Stockholm on his way to the North Cape. He had heard of the remarkable men who could walk under the water and was anxious to try it himself. One day near the end of October, Negri borrowed a small boat and went out the few metres to the salvage. Negri described the divers' all-leather uniform: coat, trousers and boots. Iron rings and string made the uniform reasonably watertight. Struck with wonder, he watched the diving bell and its diver being lowered into the water. After a quarter of an hour, it was rais-

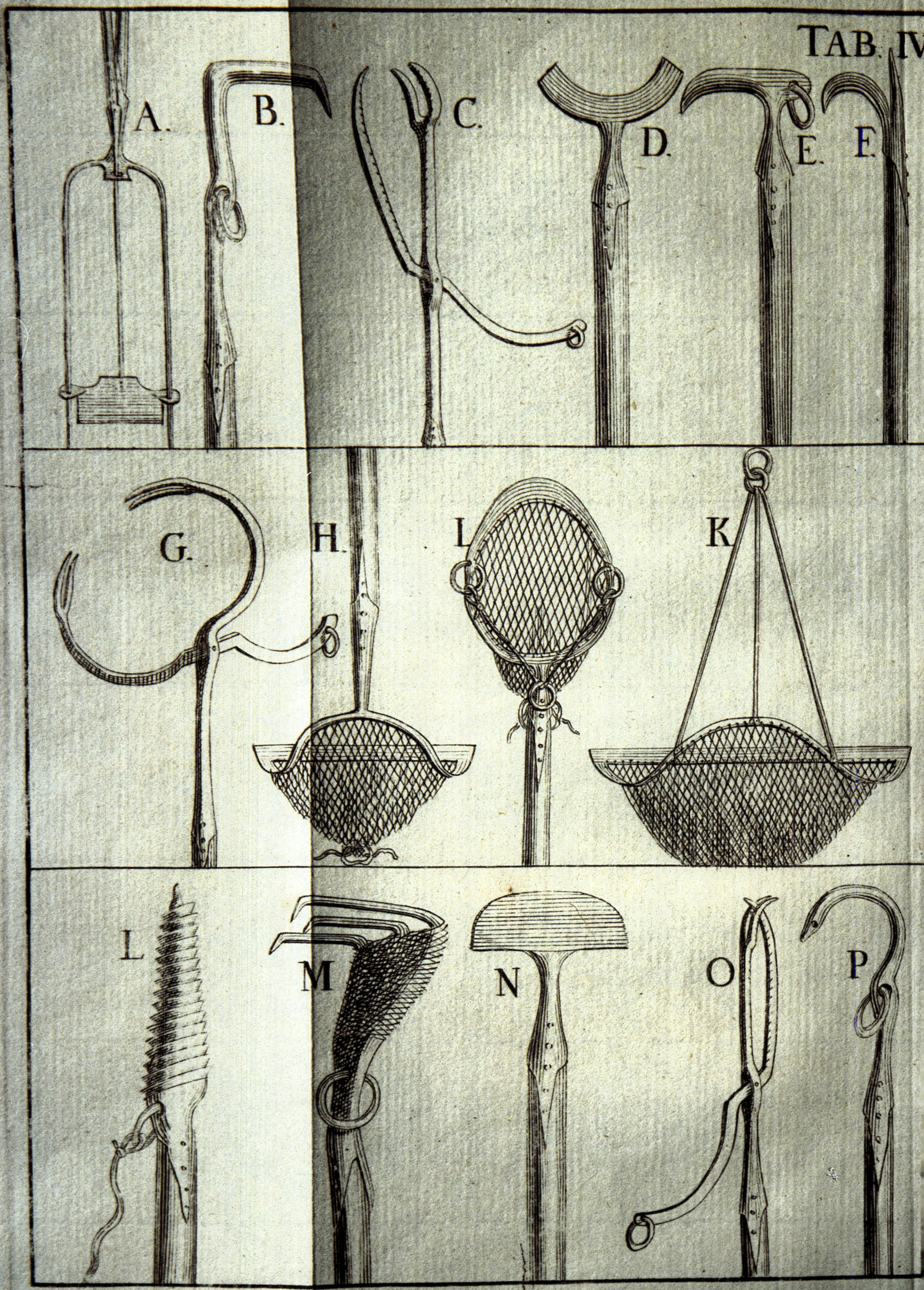
TAB. IV.
A.
B.
C.
D.
E.
F.
G.
H.
I.
K.
L.
M
N
O
P

ed. A cloud of steam exited the bell and the diver shivered from cold. Negri said he asked how long the diver could stay on the sea bottom. A half-hour, he reportedly answered. "I decided not to try," Negri confessed, "to protect my health".

The salvaging of the Vasa's cannon continued for two years from 1663. It was extremely risky work, especially since the salvagers were experimenting with extending the dive time. Diver Anders was bedridden, coughing blood, for eight days after he was made to breathe air through a long tube. Lars and Olof, two divers from Gothenburg, arrived in Stockholm in 1663 and were told to start work immediately. They had been making dives for von Treileben for five years, but now became slightly anxious. "We wouldn't have come if we knew we had to start right away," they told their employer. It was February and freezing cold.

By 1665, divers had hoisted up more than fifty of the ship's sixty-four cannon. Von Treileben and Peckel were now squabbling over money and quit.

In 1683 yet another adventurer tried his luck. Liberton, as he was called, succeeded in salvaging one cannon. But sixty years on the seabed had severely damaged the metal. Liberton tried unsucessfully to sell it to the navy. "Whatever you may have brought up from the Vasa you are free to sell to whomever you will," was the depressing answer. Liberton gave up. The Vasa had become worthless.

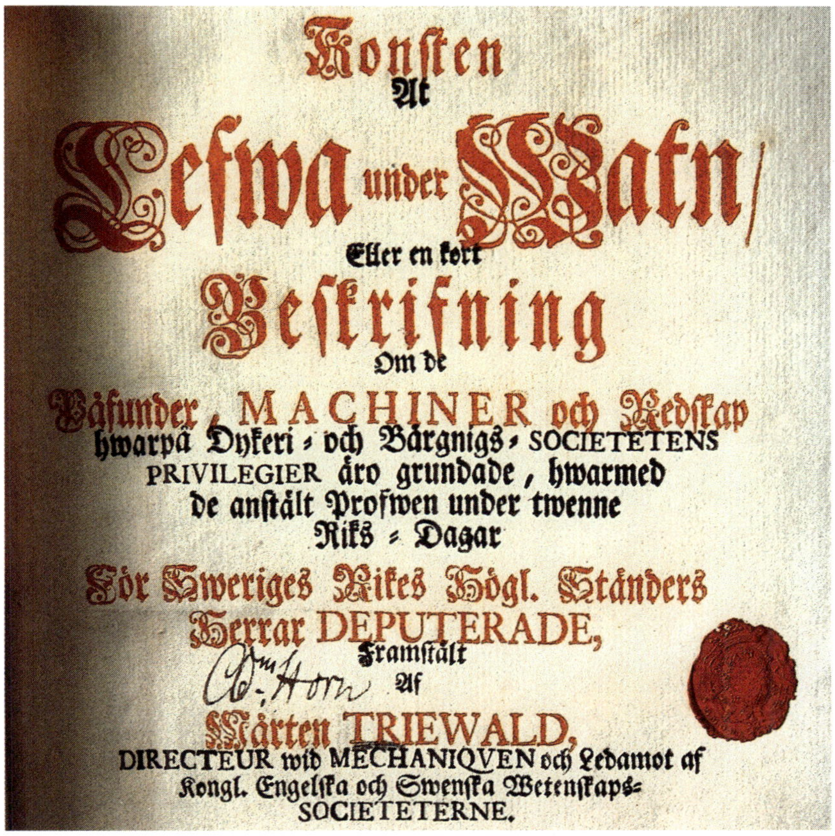
Konsten
At
Lefwa under Watn/
Eller en kort
Beskrifning
Om de
Påfunder, MACHINER och Redskap
hwarpå Dykeri- och Bärgnigs- SOCIETETENS
PRIVILEGIER äro grundade, hwarmed
de anstält Profwen under twenne
Riks-Dagar
För Sweriges Rikes Högl. Ständers
Herrar DEPUTERADE,
Framstält
Af
Mårten TRIEWALD,
DIRECTEUR wid MECHANIQVEN och Ledamot af
Kongl. Engelska och Swenska Wetenskaps-
SOCIETETERNE.

"The Art of Living Under The Waters" was the title of a book by inventor Mårten Triewald. Its publication date was more than half a century after the Vasa's cannon had been salvaged. However, 17th-century divers probably used similar primitive hooks and pincers to those Triewald recommended.

The Salvage

EXTRAORDINARY MEN and women and strong personalities have, for better and for worse, shaped the destiny of the warship Vasa. Gustavus Adolphus, to take the prime example, who interfered with the construction process and whose fault it most probably was that the ship was built unstably. And Dame Brita of Ängsö who sold the timber the Vasa was made from. And Admiral Fleming, who did nothing to stop the ship sailing. Master Shipbuilder Henrik Hybertsson, as well, who built the ship in record time. And Albrecht von Treileben, who salvaged the cannon.

Then, for three hundred years, the proud but worthless ship was forgotten by all but a few marine history researchers. And there were skippers who would curse whatever it was that was snaring their anchors off Beckholmen island in Stockholm's inner harbour. The researchers had little idea of where the Vasa lay; neither did the skippers know what their anchors were getting caught in. No one really cared. No one except a remarkably stubborn young engineer called Anders Franzén. Which brings us to the early 1950s.

A man, a boat and a plumb weight. Anders Franzén found the Vasa at the bottom of Stockholm harbour in 1956. It lay between Beckholm island and Tegelvik bay. Franzén made his discovery after exhaustive studies of archive material and many hours alone with a map and a lead weight on the harbour waters.

Franzén was another of these extraordinary people. He even had a motto: "See what everyone has seen and think what no one has thought." Franzén saw and thought: 1. The Baltic Sea is unique since ship-worms cannot survive in its brackish water. This worm is actually a tiny shellfish *Teredo navalis* that will consume everything of wood in saltier seas. 2. The Baltic is unique in that it has had a bustling maritime traffic for millennia. 3. The Baltic is uniquely difficult to navigate, which means that there have been countless shipwrecks.

Anders Franzén and the core sampler he used in his quest for the Vasa.

Thus: many ships must be lying intact on the Baltic seabed like frozen moments or time machines. The time machine Franzén chose to study was the Vasa. He went back through the records to the fateful date of 10 August 1628. The sources did not give the exact position of the shipwreck, so Franzén drew up maps and marked possible locations. He then did what archivist researchers seldom or never did at the time: he went out into the real world. He rowed out into the main body of water in Stockholm harbour, Strömmen, with grappling irons and maps, looking for the unfortunate ship.

On 25 August 1956 he got a real bite. His home-made lead weight with a core sampler at the end caught in something and came up filled with a bit of blackened oak. The spot was just off the dock of Beckholmen island. A few days later, diver Per Edvin Fälting went down and could confirm Franzén's suspicions.

Franzén and Fälting became two of the main figures in the second part of the

The principle figures in the salvage of the Vasa were Per Edvin Fälting and Anders Franzén. Fälting, a diver, led the underwater team. Franzén lobbied the Royal Family, the navy, business leaders, media, government and the general public.

A little shellfish called "Teredo navalis", or ship's worm, destroys wood quickly. It thrives in saltwater but is not found in the brackish Baltic Sea. This has led to the unique preservation of many wooden ships on the Baltic seabed.

Vasa's saga. Franzén, the discoverer, thought what no one else did: he wanted to do what had not been possible in the 17th century – hoist up the entire ship. Fälting, the diver, who had twelve thousand hours underwater by the time the Vasa was discovered, became The Diver for all of Sweden and an appreciable part of the world around, since the Vasa quickly became an international news story. Newspapers, radio, newsreels and the newest medium, television, hung on every development of the salvage operation.

The work was done by naval divers most used to heavy work. They were cut from the same cloth as Diver Anders and the other men who, 350 years earlier, were walking under water. The Vasa was like a battered paling fence, with beams, planks and other flotsam catching easily on the divers' air and safety lines. The Vasa dive demanded skill and great caution. Fälting's advice to young divers going down to the ship for the first time could have been uttered in the 17th century: "If you feel like you're dying down there in the cold and dark, drop what you're doing and find out what has gone wrong." The divers dug – or rather, flushed – six tunnels under the wreck. The question the salvage crew, museum officials and Franzén were faced with was whether the thousand-tonne hull would hold. The divers working under the ship had the same thought on their minds. Luckily, no serious accidents occurred during the salvage.

Even before the Vasa was lifted, the ship had been forced to give up part of its

After salvage work, the Vasa was so watertight that it could float unaided. It was then hauled into dock where the archaeological investigation was to take place.

Onboard the Vasa, time stopped on 10 August 1628. 333 years later, archaeologists were able to walk right into the 17th century. They found hapless victims who went down with the ship, the crew's personal effects, food and weapons. The thick anchor cable was also still there.

Salvage work on the Vasa was complicated. Tunnels for the lifting cables had to be dug under the ship. The collapsed stern had to be reinforced and rebuilt. 6000 iron bolts had rusted away and the holes they left had to be plugged. The navy's best divers did most of the work.
(next pages)

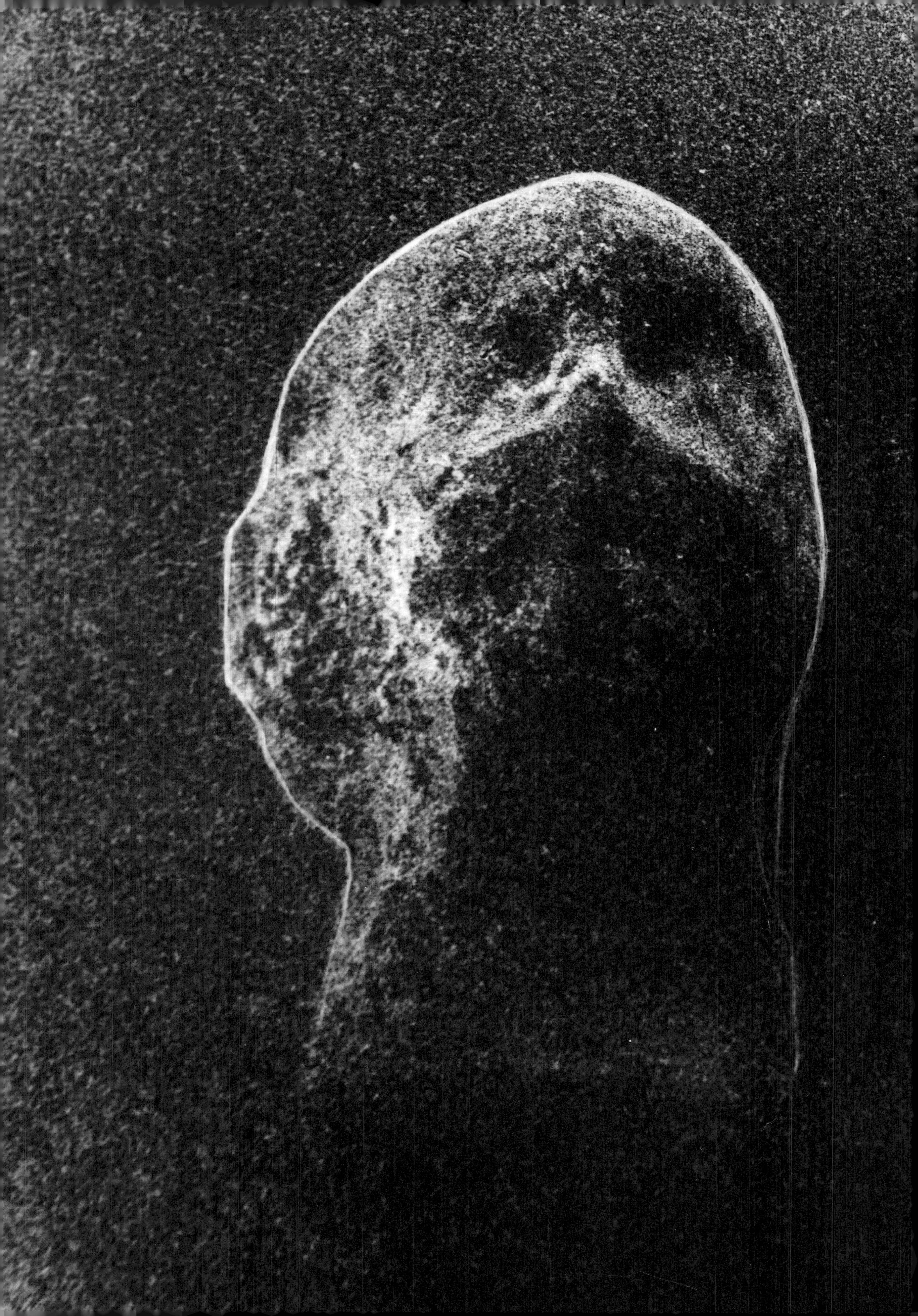

In the Vasa Museum, the bowsprit and parts of the upright rigging have been replaced on the ship.

The simple wooden bowls and spoons of the seamen have survived better than the officers' pewter service. The wooden spoons and bowl shown here were found together. Several seamen ate from the same bowl. This pewter box contained remnants of butter.

treasure trove. From the depths came lions, mermaids, human skulls and cannon.

The tunnelling work took two years. At the end of August 1959 it was time to lift the ship. The Neptun company positioned pontoons over the Vasa, threaded cables through the six tunnels, and lifted the old hull just a fraction from the seabed. The ship was towed to shallower waters in sixteen stages. On 24 April 1961, it was time for the final lift. After 333 years, the warship Vasa broke the surface.

On board the Vasa, time had stopped at five o'clock on the afternoon of 10 August 1628. Following the salvaging, archaeologists were allowed into the time machine. They dug, flushed and sifted their way through the black goo that filled the entire ship – a goo full of memories from 1628. Fourteen thousand items were registered in the five months'-long archaeological dig. They found seamen's chests filled with provisions, clothes and small personal momentoes. They found meat barrels in the hold and the seaman who had been trapped under a cannon mounting when the ship keeled over. They found the admiral's table in his cabin, with butter in a box and medicinal rum in a tin flask. They found the crew's simpler plates and wooden spoons and the officers' beautiful tin service.

The helmsman had stayed at his post. His remains lay beside the steering whipstaff. The ship's cat was still on board, as well as her prey – black rats.

A competition was held to choose the design for the Vasa Museum. The winning entry was by the Hidemark & Månsson Company. The building was placed over an old dry dock and the masts lead visitors to the museum. It is only a few hundred metres from where the Vasa was built.

BETWEEN THE PILLARS OF HERCULES

At the beginning of the 17th century, a static worldview crumbled. Knowledge was power. Common sense and experience were the lodestars. But consumption was still being treated with the ashes of a cuckoo and dysentery with snake meat.

Vol 2
MEDIOCRIA
FIRMA
Multi pertransibunt & augebitur scientia.
MONITI MELIORA

The Great Renewal

A SHIP IS RUNNING before the wind between the Pillars of Hercules in the Straits of Gibraltar on the title page of the English philosopher Francis Bacon's unfinished work, *The Great Renewal* (*Instauratio magna*). The year is 1620. The ship is sailing with a strong, stable wind and is under foresail, mainsail and mizzen. Flags flap from the masts and the wide world is waiting. It is beyond the straits and the pillars Hercules placed there, according to mythology. One of his great works was to prise apart the Atlas Mountains and join the Mediterranean and the Atlantic. Now, the good ship Common Sense was out to do more great works and conquer the world.

Bacon's message was that knowledge is power, and only through observing, describing and systematising reality could mankind improve its lot. Common sense and experience were the lodestars. Nature was unfathomable and progress was promised to those who could investigate it with the right methods. Experiment, exhorted Bacon, but philosophers are themselves not always good researchers. His own experiments were questioned and he died of pneumonia after studying whether freezing could preserve birds. Ice and salt solution killed the philosopher. This was in 1626. But Francis Bacon's philosophy was pioneering. Man would dominate nature using experience and experimentation. Nature should be at the service of man, said Bacon, and give us a better, richer life. Seventeenth-century researchers made many new and remarkable discoveries and were justifiably convinced that even more surprising ones awaited.

The title page of Francis Bacon's great work, The Great Renewal. The ship running before the wind between the Pillars of Hercules symbolises philosophy's belief in the future. "Knowledge is power," wrote Bacon and encouraged his contemporaries to enbark on voyages of discovery – on the Seven Seas, in nature and in the laboratory.

Francis Bacon saw this development as good per se, since its driving force was the selfless wish to promote mankind's temporal well-being. Here, his judgement was faulty, since so many inventions and discoveries of the time were produced through interplay between commerce and the natural sciences. This was what propelled the maritime powers – England, Holland, Spain, Portugal and France – with the same momentum as the ship passing between the Pillars of Hercules.

"Wonderful! It is wonderful," rejoiced the Swedish educator Nicolaus Andreas Granius in a letter sent from Prague in late 1610 after having heard that a professor from Padua, using a rare eyeglass, had discovered four satellites orbiting Jupiter. The rare glass was the first astronomical telescope and the Paduan professor was Galileo. News spread quickly even in the early 17th century. It had only been a year since the Dutchman Jan Lippershey accidentally discovered that a vane looked bigger and seemed to be closer when looked at through a concave and a convex lens. This gave astronomers, navigators and military field command-

Danish astronomer Tycho Brahe studied the planets, stars and meteors from the island of Ven in the strait between Sweden and Denmark. His mathematical calculations formed the basis for the theories of Galileo and Kepler in the early 17th century.

This celestial globe from Holland was signed in 1625.

LEO
Hydra
Crater
Corvus

ers an extraordinary tool – the telescope. Scientists and astrologers, such as Denmark's Tycho Brahe, who had earlier studied the heavens had been unable to enlarge and reinforce light and pictures. They were forced to place their trust in the naked eye. Using his new telescope, Galileo took only a few months to discover the mountains on the moon and Jupiter's four brightest moons. But the telescope was only one example of the progress made by the natural sciences in that century that turned upside down the worldview established by Aristotle almost two thousand years earlier. A few others: Using observations made by Brahe, his German pupil Johannes Kepler calculated that the planets moved around the sun in elliptical, not circular, orbit. He also studied the fragmentation of light through lenses, both mechanical and human. Galileo Galilei, the Italian,

The City of Augsburg presented Gustavus Adolphus with a magnificent chest of wonders.

Students of science were praising the progress of knowledge while folklore lived on. For example, most common people still believed the seas to be populated with sea creatures similar to humans.

investigated the motion of falling bodies and of the pendulum and also posed questions about the reasons for tidal movement. Englishman William Harvey discovered the circulation of blood in 1628. Dutchman Christiaan Huygens described centrifugal force and the wave theory of light as well as developing the pendulum clock and making navigation at sea safer by constructing more reliable clocks. And French mathematician Blaise Pascal invented the calculator in 1641. Swedish scientist Olof Rudbeck discovered and described lymphatic vessels in 1653 after dissecting four hundred animals. That is, unless it was the Dane Thomas Batholin who made the discovery first. He had published his findings on the bodily vessels and their white secretion several weeks before Rudbeck's discovery was made public.

"Knowledge is power" might also have served as a motto for King Gustavus Adolphus. That, or: "How Wondrous It Is to Know." It is doubtful that he knew of Francis Bacon but according to Chancellor Axel Oxenstierna, the two were kindred spirits: the King was curious about everything.

The Gustavianum at Uppsala University was built between 1622 and 1625. It housed the university's main auditorium, dining hall and student chambers. The building has been called "the Citadel of the Sun," and is topped by this globe.

He worked on the development of cannon and range tested them until they fell apart. He researched whether soap or grease was best for getting line to run smoothly on a mast. Whenever he had an hour free, he would teach soldiers to fence and storm redoubts. Warfare and its study was the air that he breathed but it was during his reign that the first maps of Sweden were drawn up, even though there were only six copies made, for fear that one might fall into enemy hands. The year was 1626, the same year Sweden's first map of the world was published. As a consequence, an Office of the Surveyor was founded in 1628.

In April 1632, Gustavus Adolphus was in Augsburg, Germany. Augsburg was the artisanship and handicraft capital of northern Europe, boasting more goldsmiths and watchmakers than bakers and butchers. There he was presented with a present that perfectly suited one so thirsty for knowledge: it was a cabinet containing a world in miniature, with all human knowledge represented.

The cabinet, now at Uppsala University, had been made according to instructions from the merchant, diplomat and collector, Philipp Hainhofer. Thirty artisans worked for seven years to fashion the cabinet and the hundreds of objects that fill the cunning drawers and compartments. There was everything, from an auto-dulcimer to blown glass, human hide, snakes, telescopes, amber apples, works of art, caskets of balsam and mathematical instruments. The cabinet had nature specimens and a miniature birdhouse. Five falcons were prisoners, and round the foot of each were a ring and a bangle. There were games of chess, backgammon and cards.

Action Most Noble

CHANCELLOR AXEL OXENSTIERNA is lying in a coffin, quiet and still, and with his feet bound, in a church in Jäder in the province of Södermanland, immediately south of Stockholm. Such a man of action would walk away, if at all possible, so they had tied his feet together with linen tapes when he was buried in 1654. The French cardinal Mazarin once said of Sweden's most influential man (with the possible exception of the King): "He is a bottomless source of well-spoken advice and should all of Europe's ministers be found on the same vessel, the rudder should be granted to the Swedish chancellor." For Axel Oxenstierna, for the King and for the nobles, action was all-important. To act was to live and to live was to act. Or, as it is written on a wall at Skokloster castle: "The most handsome side of a man is his actions."

Hunting was an important part of the education of a young nobleman, building such important character traits as courage and the ability to act. Hunting weapons were often richly decorated.

Axel Oxenstierna's willingness to take action and his analytical prowess were admired by statesmen throughout Europe.

A hunting scene on a ceiling at Kalmar castle. (next pages)

The urge to act was a prerequisite for Sweden's transformation from small, unimportant, old-fashioned country in the north to European Great Power. The men of action around the King and Oxenstierna recognised the need for better education, better weapons, better ships, better roads, better postal service, better tax collection, better priests, better soldiers, better towns – better everything.

To achieve all this, more money was needed and more iron, more copper, more silver, more tar, more grain, more timber, more soldiers and even more money. But also more consensus and unity.

This is where the wise Oxenstierna began. In most European countries there was a continuous battle between the monarch and the higher nobility. The chancellor saw the destructiveness in this lack of concord and likened Sweden to a ship in danger. If those on board, both of high and low birth, did not "in unity apply themselves to their tasks" the ship would founder.

This was the genesis of what has become known as the Swedish Model: a prearranged distribution of power between, at this time, king and high nobility. But the other estates also had important jobs on the Swedish ship of state. And besides, they dared to make their voices heard – and the King and his councillors listened! Sweden was already a more egalitarian country than others in Europe. There were, for example, no serfs and no bailiffs who held the population in terror.

The King and councillors approached their task of changing the country with eagerness bordering on obsession. The first goal was a strong nation with a strong army. The commitment was amazing. All the country's reserves, both human and natural resources, were called on.

Unity and total control of the population were of paramount importance. Only

The first reasonably accurate map of Sweden was drawn by Andreas Bureus in 1626. Yet the mythical island of Gunnars öra was still shown (top centre).

The growing of flax was encouraged. Linen was worn next to the skin and was believed to rub dirt away.

Artisans moved to Sweden from the continent and Swedes brought home utility goods from their travels or as spoils of war. The early 17th-century plates and knives are British.

with those goals achieved could taxes be called in and soldiers demobilised. Swedes have always been good at keeping each other in line and the King now called on the clergy for help. They were given the job of drawing up lists of all who lived in each parish, both old and young. This is how Sweden came to have the world's oldest census records – to the delight of modern genealogists and of the authorities in the 17th century.

Using the priests' lists, taxes could be levied with previously unknown efficiency. In the ten years from 1618 to 1628, tax revenues increased by fifty percent. Earlier, only farmers who owned their own property were taxed. Now, all who worked for him owed taxes to king and country: farmhands, serving girls and the proletariat. There were other, supplementary, taxes: mill tax, cattle tax, property tax and customs tariffs of the most varied kinds.

The census lists were also used to create a cheap army. Every tenth man was designated a soldier. Ideally, he should be "in his prime years," between 18 and 30. This was an effective way to avoid induction of professional soldiers and mercenaries who were expensive and who demanded payment in pure silver.

Fresta
Åker
Stockholm
Teby
Sueuskehöga
Nijsker
Moian
Malkubben
Böirneskär
Gunnarsöra
Horsten
Sandö Sampn
Aspöö
Nemdön
Nosten
Hundskär
Uto
Ornon
Elsnabben
Runö
Wijksten
Gunnarsten
Lands ort
Gotske Sandö
Faro
Slythamn
Oestergard
Wisby
Sanuijk
Noruijk
Gottlandia
Hoborg
HICVM

But a strong army needed good, well-trained officers. There was no problem in recruiting to the higher ranks. Following ancient tradition, they were drawn from the noble families, The problem was among the lower commissioned ranks. A certain level of education was needed, although not at university level and not necessarily academic. "What is an academic?" asked Chancellor Axel Oxenstierna rhetorically, answering: "A shirt, a pair of trousers and a few books." The King realized that the answer lay in a broader-based school system, even if it was to take centuries for the idea to be given a lasting application.

The new taxes and tariffs proved insufficient to fund all the changes that were necessary, or the wars to be fought. "Other states wage war when they are rich," said Johan Adler Salvius. "Sweden does when it is poor." Salvius realised that working in the King's office demanded almost universal knowledge, so he studied law, medicine and theology. The wars waged until the early 1630s, when Swedish military success finally allowed the army to feed itself (by pillaging land it had conquered), were wars on credit. Even up to mid-1631, the King was in desperate need of money and wrote to his chancellor that if money was not sent by return of post, then he did not know what he would do, "since We are now completely bereft of monies, neither have Our riders received monies for months and have had to sustain themselves by robbery."

Commerce was also undeveloped. Life in Sweden was based on self-sufficiency and the country's exports were modest and export income equally so. The reason

Copper and iron became Sweden's most important export products. Large, attractive mills and mines appeared in south central Sweden, but there were also many small and primitive blast furnaces and smithies. The photograph is of the Vira Mill in the region of Uppland and the drawing is of the copper mine at Falun in Dalarna province.

was partly that Swedish aristocrats should not, according to contemporary codex, indulge in trade. A noble was a public official or an officer, not a shopkeeper. The King even talked of the "great contempt" that existed for aristocrats who ran businesses and thereby competed with merchants and burghers.

In consequence, many of the lower aristocratic families were poor to the point of ruin, some so poor that they were given dispensation from attendance at meetings of the *riksdag*, or parliament, in Stockholm. And when councillors Per Sparre and Mattias Soop invited foreign visitors to dinner, the latter were surprised to find themselves in a dining room without wall-coverings. "And," wrote an astonished Frenchman, "over the table hung a blue cloth to prevent spiders falling in our food."

Conditions were different for noble women. The main reason was the many wars being fought. For long periods, the women were forced to manage farms and properties on their own. Canny and resourceful mistresses ran many mansions. They ran the properties but often also built up sizeable enterprises.

"A man is a wife's head," as the saying went, but the court records of the day show that it was common for a husband to will his house and fortune to his wife. One such will from 1629 begins: "First, let this letter proclaim that my lovely and beloved wife Margareta Persdotter shall, upon my death, retain all that I own of goods and chattels as long as she should live."

With heads of families buried in the clay of Germany or Poland, widows gained independence and greater freedom to act. Often, they were tempted not to abandon this freedom. On the board of the powerful Copper Company sat not only Chancellor Axel Oxenstierna and the well-known Louis De Geer but also Miss Agnes of Holstein; when the shipbuilders needed oak for the Vasa, they turned to Dame Brita Bååt in Stockholm's lake valley; when Master Shipbuilder Henrik Hybertsson died, his wife, Margareta, took over his vital position at the naval shipyard. "I must fulfil the contract my dear departed husband agreed to," she said as if it were self-evident. The best-known example is Maria Sophia De la Gardie, who was widowed at the age of 21. She began paper production, flour milling, glove making and coal mining on her various properties. She organised, produced and traded – and successfully managed her fortune.

All this was far from enough for the country's progress. Sweden needed outside help to kick-start proper trade and export. Backers and expertise were to be found in the leading nations of western Europe. Those who arrived on this errand were mainly the Dutch, Germans and Scots. Families such as the De Geers, the De Besches, the Mommas and the Kruses immigrated to Sweden, bringing with them

A mine gallery at the Sala silver mine. Iron from the Bergslagen region, copper from Falun and silver from Sala were among Sweden's most important material resources. Iron and copper provided export income and skilled mining engineers and smiths were enticed to Sweden to help develop the mining industry. Many were Walloons from the Spanish Netherlands, today's Belgium.

a retinue of professionals. Cash flowed in and, in exchange, the foreign bankers, merchants and entrepreneurs acquired properties, forests, mines, mills and titles. These were the Europeans who got Sweden's mines and mills going and who helped Sweden make proper money from its exports for the first time. The main moneymaker was copper; Sweden was alone in Europe in possessing large, accessible copper reserves and Falun copper was made into coins and cannon in many countries. Never before had so many fires burned in the mines in south central Sweden; never before had so much charcoal been burned; never before had so much iron, silver and copper been produced.

The Falun copper mine, as described by the Frenchman Ogier in 1634: "Here, the ice melts partly on its own and partly through the agency of fires lit by mine-workers, providing a trickle of rain to walk through. It is a sight both wonderful and dreadful, these caves where flames shine and flash along the walls, thawing and eating into the rock."

But it was obvious that everything was done in a hurry. The cannon that divers brought up from the Vasa were crude and badly polished. It was the same with the copper coins of the time. Manufacture had been simplified so much that the coins were being made square instead of round. They were called clips, and you would often find double imprints and uneven edges where the striker had missed and had struck an extra time with his mallet.

What did this mean to Chancellor Oxenstierna, who was an achiever yet still scrupulous? Was he convinced that the great transformation of Sweden was bound to succeed? Or did he suffer doubts? He provided his own answer: "When I see the weight, the burden, the repulsion, the disillusion, the means, the people, the enemies, the friends, the danger, the beginnings, the successes, the events and the outcome, my hair stands on end."

Cuckoo Ash and Other Remedies

IN 1628, Professor of Physiology Johannes Raicus presented his treatise on consumption to his faculty at Uppsala University. His recommended cure was a brew concocted from the ashes of a cuckoo caught before Midsummer. This was the practical application of the theories of the Swiss physician, Paracelsus (1493–1541). Like cures like. The unclean phlegm which caused consumption could be driven out with an emetic as black as soot. The same logic said that liver diseases could be cured with the liver-shaped leaves of the hepatica, and that cuts should be covered with an ointment made from the perforated leaves of St. John's wort. Appearance, taste and smell were the indicators.

When a surgeon-barber mixed his potions, the recipe was often "like heals like." The liver-shaped leaves of the blue anemone were assumed to cure liver disease. The flower's Latin name is Hepatica nobilis. Hepar means liver.

In the same year that Johannes Raicus was treating consumption with cuckoo ash, the Englishman William Harvey was able to describe the circulation of the blood. Harvey arrived at his discovery through dissection and actual study of the human body. This was relatively new, in relation to both the ancient teaching of the body's Four Humours and to Paracelsus's like-cures-like philosophy. But

Mandrake root often resembles a human figure. This was taken to mean that the root had supernatural properties. A potion made from mandrake has narcotic qualities.

many years would pass before medical science based on a realistic description of the human body would gain currency.

It was not uncommon for a natural scientist to both conduct sensible experiments and also fiddle around with magic decoctions and pure mythology. The Flemish scientist Jan Baptista van Helmont discovered carbonic acid but also described how mice could germinate from cheese and dirty laundry.

For people in general, but also for most of those with university degrees, it was accepted that nature's invisible powers commanded us, and that these powers had to be conquered. In 1623, half the population of Stockholm died from the plague and several other epidemics struck the city and the country in the same decade. The professor who used cuckoo ash on consumption patients wrote about the bubonic plague. He saw the disease as a divine punishment; according to the professor, murderous angels flinging lightning flashes of arsenic into the human body spread the contagion.

There was a huge difference between the theories of university-educated doctors and the bloody work of a field surgeon, amputating the limbs of sword- and bullet-wounded soldiers.

The doctor's most important tools were the works of Hippocrates and Galen and their thousand-year-old medical teachings based on the idea of four bodily fluids in imbalance. The cure was bloodletting, leechcraft or giving enemas. The patient was to vomit, bleed, sweat or purge the evil from his body.

The worst epidemic of the age was the plague. Black rats, also known as ship's rats, spread it. Some of these have gnawed at one of the books Nils Nilsson Brahe brought home from studies abroad in the 1650s.

It was vital to rid the body of unclean fluids, according to contemporary medicinal theory. This was done by leeching and bloodletting. "A hideous spectacle," in the eyes of one witness. These leeching glasses and bloodletting tools belonged to King Gustavus Adolphus.

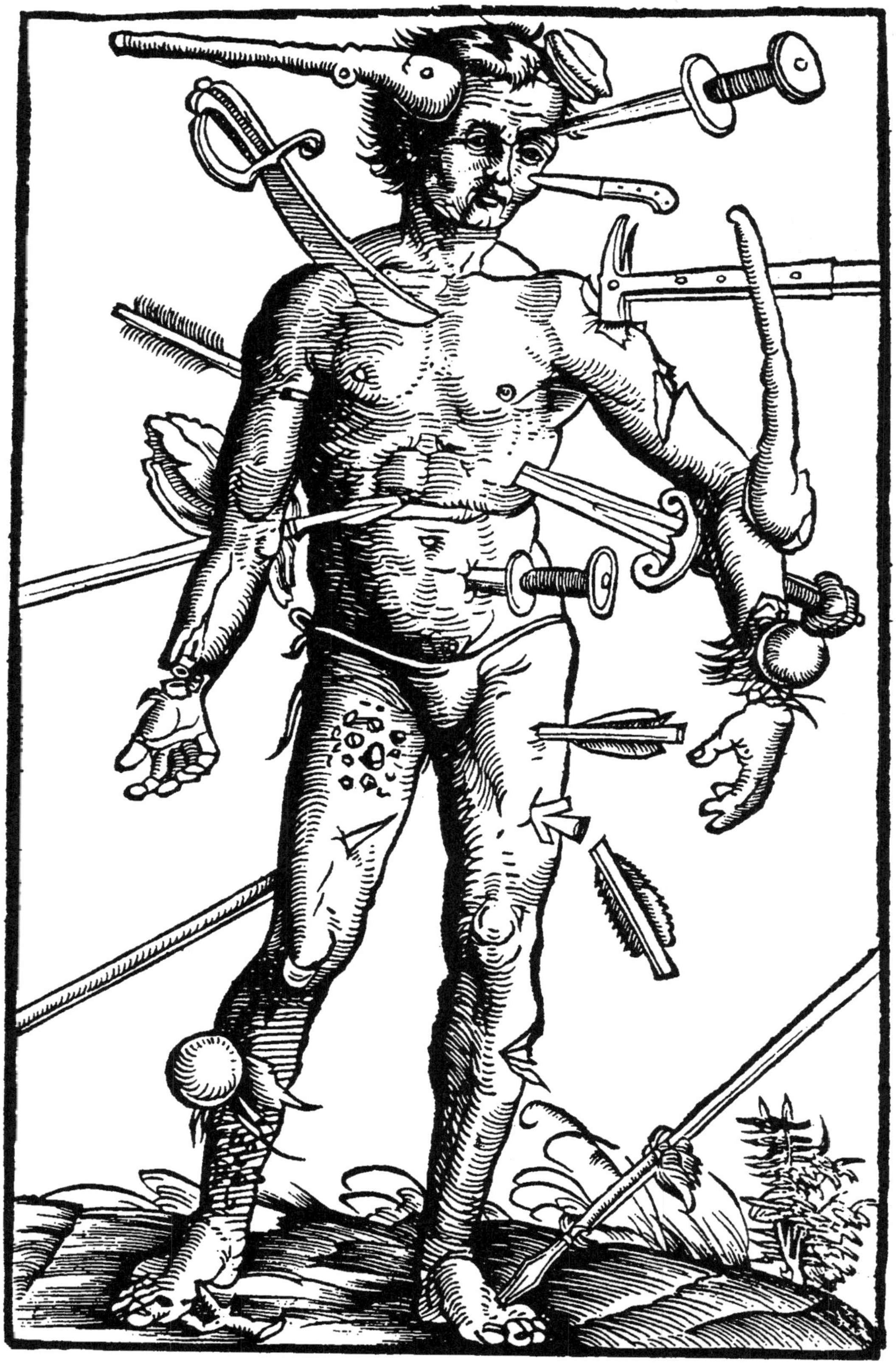

Military surgeons were known as barbers. They cut hair, pulled teeth and amputated limbs. Their tools were knives, saws and chisels. The only anaesthetic was a tourniquet bound tightly above the injury. The illustrations in contemporary medical books were gruesomely realistic.

¶ Mit dißem instrumēt solt du die hirnschal wider vffraben wañ sye ingeschlagen ist/vñ ein teyle vndersich sycht/ vnd das ander übersich. vñ magst dz thůn mit dißē instrument oben vnd neben od' hinden. Die vnderē lappen die vff dē haubt ston die sollen in gleychē gon dz man sye setzen mag wohin man wil. vnd sol das strublin do mit du in die hirnschal borest od' strubest gar scharpff sein / wie dañ hye verzeychnet ist.

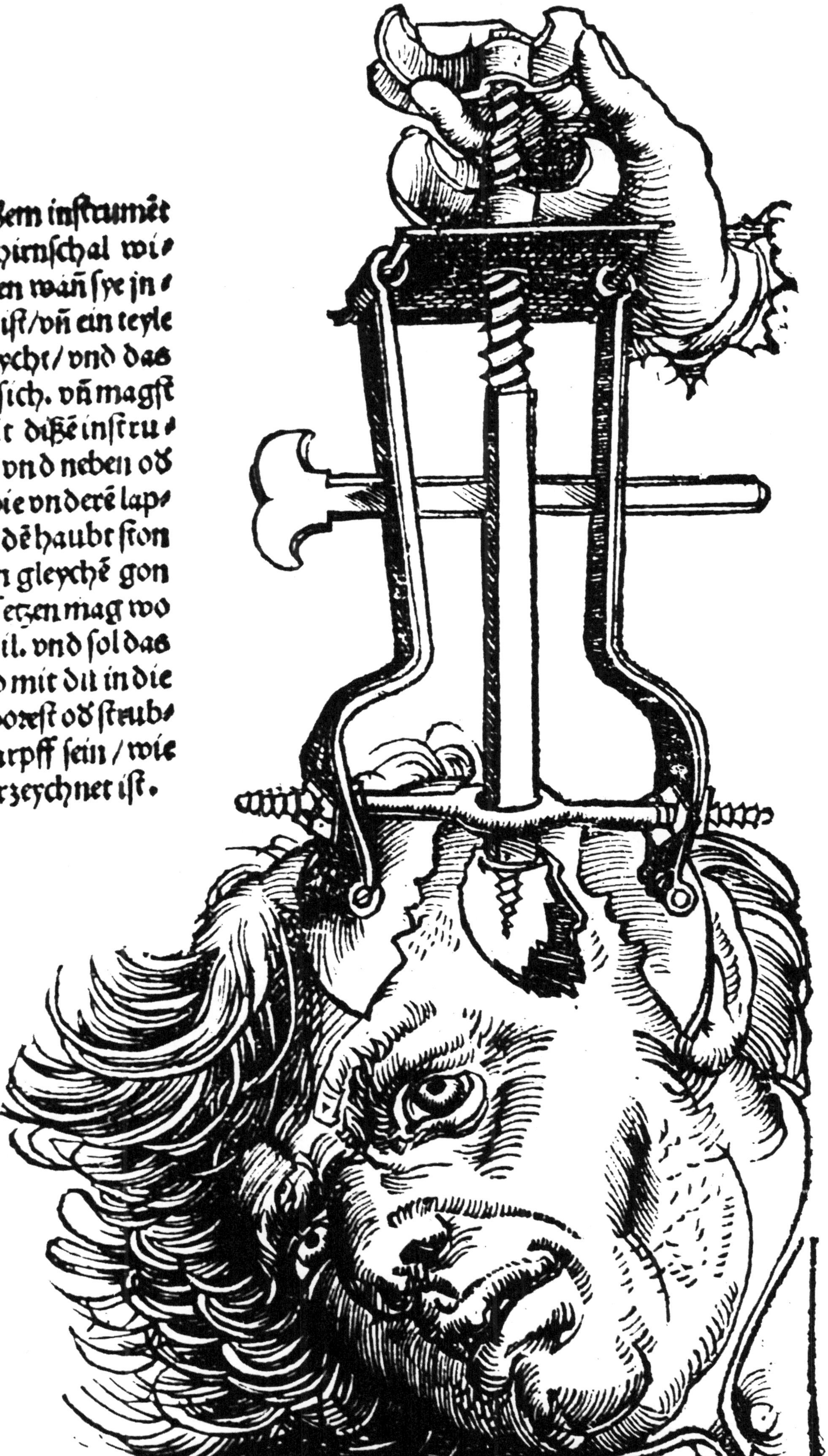

The field surgeon's most important tools were his knives, saws, scissors, tooth pliers, braces, branding irons and schnapps for anaesthetic. It was symptomatic that field surgeons were called barber surgeons in the 1600s. They trimmed beards *barba* in Latin and *Bard* in German) and hair when they were not patching up the wounded.

The medicinal arts were also practised in bathhouses. Sweating in the sauna was good for driving out malign bodily fluids and there were other services on offer, such as bloodletting and enemas. The bathers' guild emblem was a broom and a bedpan.

The atmosphere in a public sauna was not for the faint-hearted. Bleeding cups hung like parasites on the bathers and blood, sweat and water ran from them in torrents. It was "a disgusting spectacle," according to a visitor from abroad.

The diseases of the time had evocative names: "blood soot," "bone sickness," the quake, the shivers ... These days, they would be known as dysentery, malaria, diphtheria and scurvy. Disease was most rife among soldiers and sailors. The risk of infection was high and the rations, hygiene and equipment worthless. "The sol-

A simple barber's kit was found aboard the Vasa. The mortar and pestle were important; herbs and spices were ground to make powders and pills. The kit also held a tapping-cock with rooster ornamentation, a grating iron, a pewter flask, a whisk, wooden ladles and a stone jar.

diers are dying like dogs," wrote the King from Livonia in 1626, referring to illness rather than warfare. Twenty-seven soldiers were commandeered from the parish of Bygdeå in Västerbotten province and after three months of field service only one was left alive. The others had died of blood soot.

"We have won land from others but ruined our own," wrote an eyewitness. "The land is so poverty-stricken that you can journey through three or four parishes and not see a single farmhand."

Conditions were similar in the fleet. "When a ship has been at anchor for a couple of months, half the crew will have been thrown overboard," that is, buried at sea, reported Chancellor Axel Oxenstierna. Without a shot being fired.

The disease that most ravaged the army and navy was blood soot. Its symptoms were slimy, bloody diarrhoea, fever and headache. The death rate was terrifyingly high. Today, the diagnosis would probably be dysentery, a colonic sickness that spreads in unhygienic conditions. Aboard ship and in field camps, hygiene was non-existent. The cure for blood soot was a variety of strange brews. A medical book from the 16th century proposed bowel cleansing – devastating treatment for a sickness whose most serious effect was dehydration. The same book also suggested a drink composed of pomegranate peel, red and white coral, Arabian rubber and dragon blood. Dragon blood is not as outlandish as it sounds; it is the resin of the *Calamus draco* fruit, which grows in the Canary Islands.

A memento mori. One side showed a head, the other a skull with a serpent slithering through the eye sockets, illustrating the passage of time. The ivory head, little more than a decimetre tall, was made in Holland at the beginning of the 17th century.

Pain in the joints and a general feeling of frailty was called bone sickness. The cure was a salve consisting of salvia, bilberry, camomile and rosemary, boiled in a good wine. Into the liquid was stirred incense, saffron, rose petal, juniper, linseed oil and "bait oil," the latter being worms left in water and warmed by the sun.

One patent remedy was "teriak," in which snake meat was the most important ingredient. Teriak also contained squill (to strengthen the heart), different spices (to provide internal warmth), an appetiser (for the stomach) and opium and valerian (to promote breathing). Teriak was sold in the markets by travelling merchants or was mixed by barbers in field camps and onboard ship.

There were simpler cures for those who could not afford these rare herbs and strange salves. The poor had "muck pharmacy" as it was called. The main ingredients were dog faeces, menstrual blood, toads and earthworms.

If anyone actually regained health, it was due more to luck and a strong physique than to the medications of the barbers. There were, in fact, doubters. Anders the Barber asked to be relieved of his position during a maritime expedition in the 1620s. He had, he wrote to the Admiralty, not been able to cure a single sick person. Request denied, came the laconic answer. He was still better than nobody.

The Compassionate Admiral

THE SUMMER OF 1628 was rainy, windy, cold and miserable. Onboard the Swedish ships patrolling the south Baltic, conditions are intolerable. The ships carry proud names, alluding to strength, beauty and history: the Tre Kronor, the Andromeda, the Oranienbom, the Enhörningen, the Papegojan and the Jungfru. But onboard there is deprivation. Their orders are to collect tariffs from the ships that sail in and out of Danzig and the other Polish ports and to keep the Polish navy bottled up.

It is doubtful whether they were able to carry out their duties. The year before, the Swedes had suffered a terrible defeat at the hands of the Polish navy. Two ships were lost and many hundreds of sailors and soldiers lost their lives. The disaster was partly blamed on poor seamanship but the main reason was, as an eyewitness wrote: "Our ships had too few people and too sick."

In the early summer of 1628, 34-year-old Henrik Fleming was promoted to vice-admiral and on 1st of July took over command of the naval force blockading Danzig. The officer relieved of his command was Admiral-of-the-Realm Carl Carlsson Gyllenhielm, as he was old, tired and sick.

Vice-Admiral Fleming immediately began bombarding King Gustavus Adolphus and Chancellor Axel Oxenstierna with letters about the conditions onboard: "Should five show some signs of recuperation, then eight fall ill again," he wrote, continuing: "The Lord knows what I shall do about them. On some, their heads and throats swell so they can neither hear nor speak. Yet others swell to be like logs. For some, their legs have shrunk at the knee joint." Master Hans, the surgeon barber, had also fallen ill and was on his death bed, as were three of the admiral's ship's boys, and most ships no longer had pilots. Soon, the admiral himself was sick, suffering from headache and chills.

There was no commiseration from his superiors. "You exaggerate," answered the King, adding: "You must be very cowardly!" As customary, the King had sent the fleet its instructions in early summer. Included was the exhortation to keep clean and eat and dress properly. In the King's words, the men should look decent should they ever chance to meet anyone and stay healthy. The latter advice was exceptionally sound but impossible to follow. Besides, conventional wisdom was that epidemics broke out because the men had not enough to do. "I believe the greatest reason for sickness among the crew is that all summer, the ships have been still and the men have done little but sleep, day and night," wrote Admiral Fleming.

Vice-Admiral Henrik Fleming (1584–1650) commanded the fleet that lay off the Polish coast in the summer of 1628. Fortuitously, he had bought a quantity of lemons for the voyage and was able to use their juice to cure the scurvy that ravaged the ships' crews.

Gun decks were dark, damp, cold and unhealthy. Daylight seeped in through the grill pattern of the ceiling grate. The risk of dying of disease was far greater than of dying in battle. (next pages)

Fleming, however, was not twiddling his thumbs. By coincidence, he took onboard a load of lemons and immediately began giving lemon juice to the men sick with scurvy. "Shortly after arriving," he wrote, "I bought a couple of hundred lemons from a Dutchman." Every day in calm weather, the compassionate admiral rowed from ship to ship with lemon juice, wine and warm beer. "It cures a sailor after five days," he noted with surprise and pleasure. This was 150 years before the Scots doctor, James Lind, conducted his famous experiments that were to show that citrus fruit cured scurvy. But the lemons were quickly finished and Admiral Fleming reported in August that there were again 290 sick cases onboard and only 120 healthy men. He wanted to call off his squadron duty and sail home.

Admiral Fleming rowed between the ships of his squadron, giving sick seamen a drink composed of lemon juice, hot wine and beer.

The flasks, of masur birch, were found on the Vasa.

The King and the admiralty were, however, implacable. Fleming and his squadron were told to continue patrolling the south Baltic until the beginning of December. When he finally returned to Sweden he had to resume his command in the army. To accuse him of cowardice, as the King did, was deeply unjust. When a colonel in the Finnish cavalry and Karelian foot soldiers, the compassionate admiral had taken all of the then Norwegian province of Jämtland 1644. He was leading a regiment of only a couple of hundred men. Henrik Fleming died in 1648, sixty years old.

GOD AND WEATHER WILLING

Journeys were seldom pleasurable. A traveller never knew when he would arrive at his destination and was at the mercies of wind, weather and his Creator. Yet in those years, tens of thousands of Swedes made long journeys. Especially seamen and soldiers.

Waiting for Wind

JOHAN HAND WAS amused and confused. Hardly had Colonel Adolf Karlsson come aboard before he began arguing, commanding and asking questions: Are there compasses? Are the gun ports properly sealed? Is there grease for the parrels? Is anyone sick with 'blood soot?' "He sounded like a captain setting sail for India," wrote Johan Hand.

His amazement was justified. The experienced-sounding Adolf Karlsson was King Gustavus Adolphus in disguise.

This actually happened on 29 April 1620 at Älvsnabben in the south of the Stockholm archipelago. The Scepter was waiting at Älvsnabben when the King had arrived in a small boat. He was incognito, wearing simple, grey clothes and insisting that he be called Adolf Karlsson. His journey was so secret that Nils Eriksson, the simple fisherman who had brought him to the ship, was not allowed to return home. He was forced to travel to Germany, which was where the King was going. The reason for his journey was to see young Princess Maria Eleonora, whom Gustavus Adolphus hoped would become Sweden's queen.

The hyperactive Adolf Karlsson spent the afternoon of 29 April hunting seabirds. "He shot a duck," wrote Johan Hand.

"He shot a duck," wrote one Johan Hand in his diary for 29 April 1620. The shooter was a man calling himself Adolf Karlsson – in reality King Gustavus Adolphus, travelling incognito to court his bride. It was probably a female eider.

Later in the day, the north wind picked up and the Scepter set sail. Eight days later, the ship dropped anchor in the lee of Rügen, in Germany. It was a slow voyage on an important errand. Three hundred nautical miles in eight days makes an average speed of two knots, or four kilometres an hour.

Comparing sailing voyages and the time they took gives us a good picture of how difficult travel was in the 17th century – in fact, until the second half of the 19th century or as long as sailing ships carried people and freight. It was impossible to know how long a sea voyage would take: a few days, a week or perhaps even a month. If there were thousands of soldiers onboard a few ships, buying supplies would have been a nightmare. Should there be food for a few days or a few months?

When Gustavus Adolphus gathered his army in 1630 for the voyage to Germany, he had fifteen thousand men and a couple of thousand horses on forty ships anchored off Älvsnabben. The King embarked on 2 June. In that season, the wind of the Baltic is most often a fresh south-westerly. This held true for early June 1630. But a south-westerly is the worst possible wind for a course down to Germany, since it is a headwind. The King did not dare beat against the wind with a gigantic fleet like that, with all the soldiers and equipment onboard. He was an experienced sailor, and he had had bad experiences before. The fleet did not set out until 17 June, arriving on the 26th. On their way, the ships anchored at the northern tip of the island of Öland to take on more supplies.

The trip from the Stockholm archipelago to Germany took four weeks. During that time, fifteen thousand men had to be given food and drink and two thousand horses needed hay.

Barrels and chests found aboard the Vasa held the remains of the crew's food supplies. Analysis of the bones has identified black grouse, fish, beef, lamb and pork.

It is hard to image the situation in the galleys for the cooks and their helpers. The galley was in the lowest part of the ship and was a simple brick fireplace with protective brick walls. There was no chimney and the smoke had to find its own way out through openings in the decks above where the cramped crew lived. The cook had to prepare food over an open fire in a big iron pot – the one on the Vasa could hold 180 litres – for more than a thousand men on the bigger ships.

The cook threw salt beef and pork or salt fish into his pot. He mixed in grain, beans and dried peas. He almost certainly used seawater for liquid. The brackish water of the Baltic made little difference – the food would have been viciously salty in any case. The result was a kind of stew, to use a flattering word for what the cook scooped into the crew's wooden bowls. Seven men, a watch, ate from the same bowl. Dry bread was also an important part of their diet.

A food warmer was found far astern in the Vasa. It had been used by the officers. Food for the crew was prepared in a large, cast-iron pot in the galley in the bottom of the ship. The pot hung over an open fire in a brick fireplace.

The blue and yellow Swedish flag at the stern of the flagship Mars in 1630. (next pages)

The salty food meant they needed vast quantities of beer. The ration was three litres per man per day. "The men must have the basic necessities and not be forced to drink saltwater, which is reason for so many falling ill," ordered the King.

At best, the men ate their fill; the nutritional value was nil, unless you count the vitamins in beer. To supplement their monotonous rations, the crew was allowed to have their own small supplies of dried and smoked meat, bread and butter. In the seamen's chests on the Vasa, archaeologists found bones belonging to cows, sheep, chickens and fish, as well as butter and alcohol, presumably rum. There was also fishing gear, such as nets, reels and cod jigging. Whenever the ship was at anchor, crewmen would be hanging over the rails or off the beakhead with their fishing lines trying for fresh fish.

Despite the gigantic problems involved in feeding crews and soldiers before leaving for Germany in 1630, the King preferred to wait in the harbour until the

wind was suitable. He had sailed the Baltic countless times and knew, just as all real sailors know, that wind and weather take precedence over everything else.

After an especially difficult voyage to Riga at the end of July 1621, the King had written: "We were at sea for three days in rain, wind and evil, dark weather, upon which our ships leaked, becoming both mast-less and sail-less, especially those carrying our cavalry."

His letter described how barrels of meat, bread and beer were smashed. As the King wrote, the food and drink was little improved by being mixed with saltwater. "You can well imagine," he wrote, "how the horses fared."

And how the soldiers and seamen fared, one would like to add. There was about a square metre of space per man onboard. The crew had to eat and try to sleep on wet decks, the ship leaking from above and below. There were no bunks; crew members slept on the deck between the cannon. They sometimes had a rug to keep out the cold. If the weather turned bad, life on the gun decks must have been hell, what with the fear, the vomit, the seawater, the smoke from the galley,

Waiting for a wind. Waiting for orders. Waiting made up a large part of the seamen's life onboard ship. Free time would be spent fishing or repairing clothes and shoes. Onboard the Vasa were fishing reels, floats and cod jigs. Many of the seamen's chests held needles and thread, shoemaker's pegs and scraps of leather.

Sweden lost a large part of its fleet in the late 1620s, not in battle but through storms, ships running aground and in adequate seamanship. The coat of arms belongs to the Ankarstjerna (Anchor Star) family, ennobled in 1688.

The bust on the deck of the Vasa is called a knight and decorated the block-sheaves.

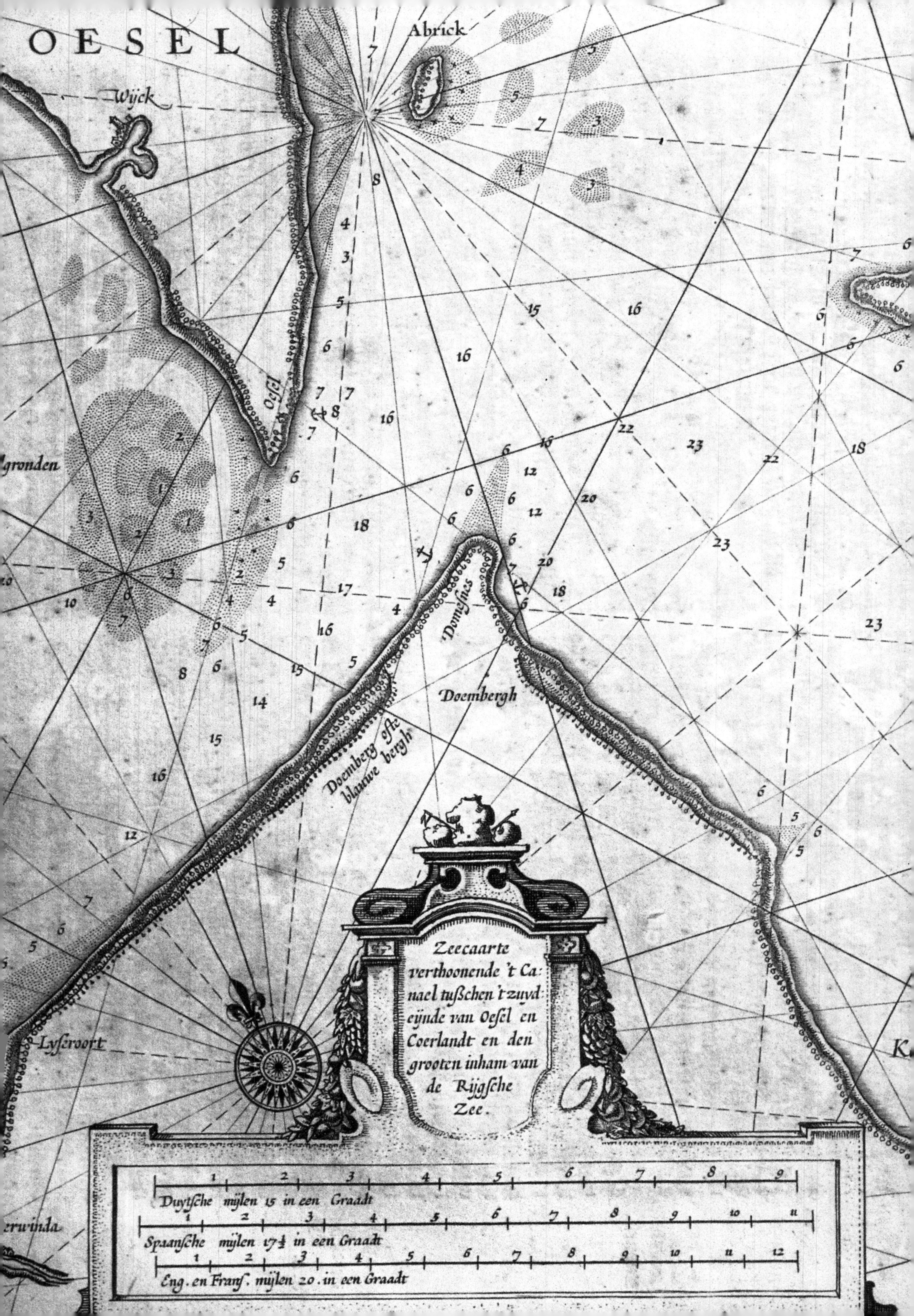
OESEL
Abrick
Wijck
Oesel
gronden
Domesnes
Doembergh
Doemberg ofte blauwe bergh
Lyseroort
Zeecaarte verthoonende 't Canael tusschen 't zuyd eynde van Oesel en Coerlandt en den grooten inham van de Rijgsche Zee.
Duytsche mijlen 15 in een Graadt
Spaansche mijlen 17½ in een Graadt
Eng. en Frans. mijlen 20. in een Graadt

the violent pitching, the crack of the sails and the crash of breaking rigging. The King reflected: "I learned just how jeopardous it is to move people in large numbers over the seas."

The sea journey to Riga in 1621 was typical of what could happen to a large fleet sailing across the Baltic with troops and equipment, and it is interesting to study what happened. At midsummer, the fleet was anchored at the naval yard in Stockholm, Skeppsgården. It was the largest fleet ever mustered by Sweden: 24 large warships, 28 smaller ones and 106 chartered cargo ships – a total of 158 ships. The fleet was ordered to Älvsnabben, an excellent harbour in the southern part of the Stockholm archipelago where fleets had gathered since the Middle Ages. The harbour is well protected from the weather and it is easy to reach the open sea using any wind but a southerly. While waiting for the fleet to arrive, the King marshalled his troops in the harbour. He had 14,000 men with whom to besiege Riga.

Navigating entry into the Gulf of Riga south of the island of Oesel is hard. There are large reefs by Domesnäs point and the shores are dangerously rocky. Swedish warships came to grief here on several occasions during the 1620s.

In favourable circumstances and before a westerly wind, a ship could sail from Stockholm to Älvsnabben in two days. If the winds were contrary, turning to the south and east, it could take a month.

Gustavus Adolphus was interested in manoeuvring and in warfare at sea, and drew up charts showing recommended ship movements.

On 10 July, three weeks later, the King and his men were still waiting for the ships. The King sent a small boat to meet the fleet, ordering Admiral-of-the-

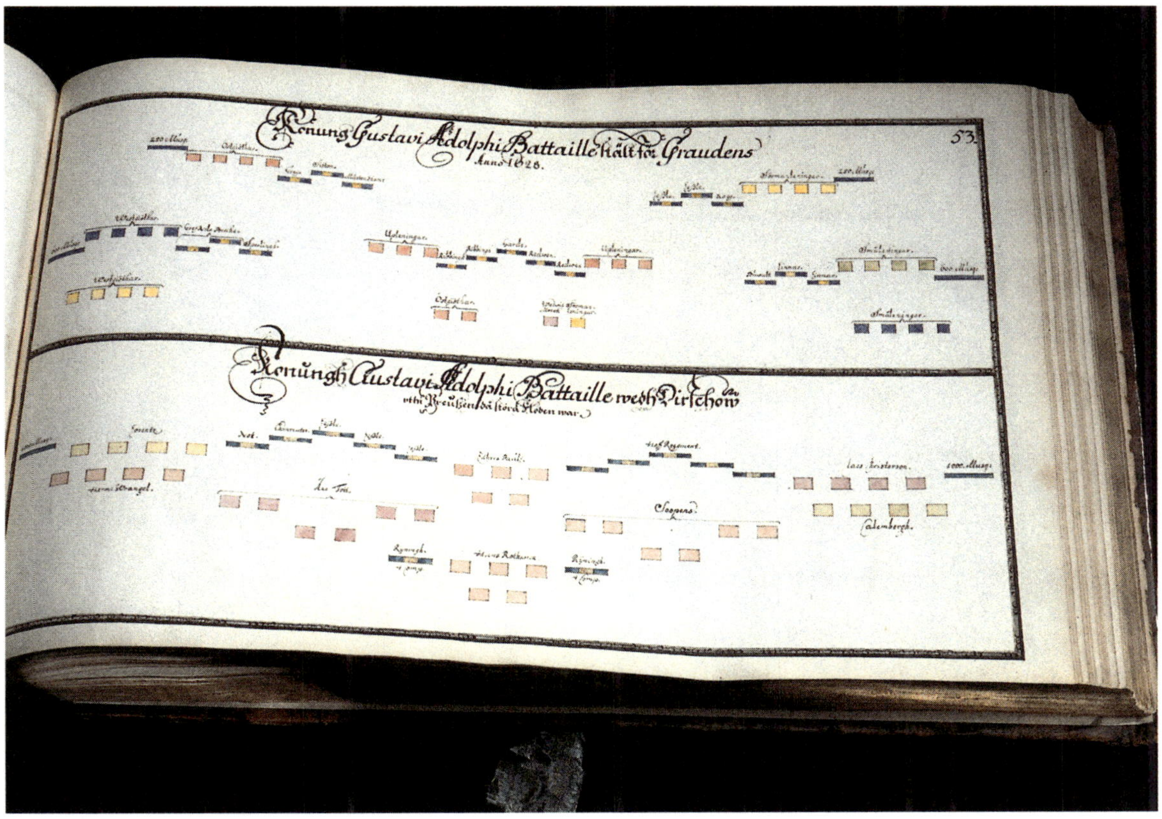

Realm Gyllenhielm to tow the ships if nothing else worked. The King wanted all 158 ships to be towed by ropes from the islands if the winds would not help. This was an impossible task, given the size of the fleet.

By this time, the fleet had covered about half the distance. The King decided on another, almost equally impracticable solution: the 14,000 soldiers were to be transported in small boats to the fleet. Against formidable odds, the operation was carried out in ten days and on 20 July, the fleet set sail. But their troubles were not over. The ten nautical miles, or 25 kilometres, to Sandhamn and the end of the archipelago took four days and the fleet did not quit the Swedish coast until 24 July. In a rising northerly wind, the ships reached the dangerous cape Domesnäs at the mouth of the Gulf of Riga after only 24 hours. By now, the wind was hard and the fleet was dispersed. The King, on the flagship Scepter, and the other large warships dropped anchor while most of the fleet did not dare sail close to land and stayed out at sea for fear of being beached.

After another 24 hours, the wind dropped. The King's ship set sail but the heavy weather returned and the ship sailed or was blown about at sea for three days and nights. The King began to worry about his horses and could only look on as supplies, beer and seawater turned into thick soup in the hold.

Shrouds and stays on the Vasa.

Approaching a coast was difficult. It was hard for large sailing ships to tack and if the wind was blowing towards land, the risk for beaching was real. "Lying waste," seamen called it. The picture is a detail of a nautical chart and shows a smaller ship approaching a coast and identifying itself by firing a signal.

On the last day of July, the Scepter finally succeeded in reaching Pernau in Livonia where the bulk of the Swedish fleet had gathered. The King then advanced on Riga by land while most of the soldiers stayed onboard the ships. A few days later, the ships sailed from Pernau to the mouth of the Düna River outside Riga. This turned out to be the only smooth and undramatic part of the voyage: eighty nautical miles without incident! But that ended on 2 August. Hard winds began blowing from the north-west – the worst possible direction for ships in the southern part of the Gulf of Riga. Ships were dragged off their anchors, lost their masts or were beached by the wind. Polish soldiers overran several.

On 4 August, the Admiral-of-the-Realm sailed up the river towards Riga. At that stage, the flagship Scepter ran aground, but could be dragged loose after cargo was taken off. Finally, on 5 August, one and half months after leaving Stockholm, the soldiers and their equipment could be off-loaded and the siege of Riga could begin.

In long voyages on the open sea, navigators used the sun, the planets and the stars. The cross-staff was a simple navigational aid. More complicated were nautical astrolabes. The one pictured is an early 17th-century Dutch model. In the small Baltic, there was little need for navigation by astronomy.

The dramatic journey of 1621 was not unique; the same thing happened over and over. Ships were becalmed, sank or were blown way off course.

The Frenchman, Ogier, set sail from Kalmar in the south to Stockholm but ran into hard weather, was blown back and had to travel by land instead. Chancellor Axel Oxenstierna wanted to sail from Stockholm to Germany. Off the island of Gotland, his ship lost part of its rigging and had to turn back. And so on.

There were several reasons for these problems.

1. The Baltic Sea is a narrow body of water with land never far off. This made it hard for large ships that were difficult to manoeuvre. There was an ever-present risk of being driven onto land.

2. The archipelagos along the Swedish and Finnish coasts were exceptionally hard to navigate for the ships of the time. It was impossible to tack in the narrow channels and ships simply had to wait for a following wind. The same was true for the narrow, shallow strait between Kalmar and Öland island.

3. In summer, the winds in the Baltic generally come from the south-west. This meant a headwind for ships sailing from Stockholm down to Germany.

4. Swedes were poorer sailors and navigators than, for example, the Dutch, the English, the Spaniards, the Portuguese and the Danes. We did not have their experience. In 1618, 4,300 Dutch ships passed through Öresund, the strait between Sweden and Denmark. The number of ships flying Swedish colours through Öresund that year was thirty.

"We set sail if it suits God and the weather," said Admiral-of-the-Realm Carl Carlsson Gyllenhielm.

Bad Roads for Fine Carriages

ROYAL COURIERS AND oyster merchants were without question to be supplied with fresh horses at inn staging posts. So a royal letter or a 'tree' of oysters (roughly 320) could reach Stockholm from Gothenburg in two-to-three days. Sometimes – at least for royal couriers – travel could take appreciably longer. The news that Gustavus Adolphus had fallen at the Battle of Lützen reached Stockholm more than a month after the event. That the King's body did not arrive in the capital until a year and a half later was because the funeral preparations were extraordinarily extensive and royal corpses, as opposed to oysters, are not perishable goods.

In the absence of snow or ice, the traveller who chose the land route was forced to ride horseback or walk. Travel by carriage was not possible even on the principle coastal road to Stockholm from Kalmar in the extreme south.
In 1642 it was decreed that there should be an inn every 20 kilometres on main roads.

For ordinary travellers without royal privileges, the journey between Stockholm and Gothenburg could take a month or more. And on top of that was the discomfort. In early 17th-century Sweden there were few roads worth the name. And travelling by coach was scarcely possible on paths that were bumpy with roots and stones and which twisted their way across the countryside, up and down over ridges and hills and through forests, over brooks, streams and rivers. There were few bridges, and fords from the Middle Ages were still in use. At best, there could be a rickety pontoon bridge of logs. Narrow planks were sometimes placed across swamps.

"Severe cold, horrifying hills, terrible horses and carriages, dreadful camps and more than awful nourishment," complained one foreign traveller.

From another perspective, it was just as bad. Until the mid-1600s, farmers were obliged to provide travellers with both horses and lodging. It was a heavy burden on those who happened to live by one of the highroads. If the traveller was carrying a royal missive, everything would be provided free of charge; others had to pay a modest sum. In a poem by Samuel Brask, Sven of Gälet bemoans his fate:

Have mercy, God, on a peasant poor
The weight of it all makes me sore
Serving and lodging plague my soul away
And the burdens grow each day
I work as long and hard as I know
But nothing in my purse does grow.

A meal cost two *öre*. As a comparison, a chicken cost six. According to the innkeeper code, an ordinary meal should consist of what "a peasant eats daily." Food like that did not often appeal to gentlefolk. The meat seemed to come from a cow that died in a ditch, complained one. If the farmer's beer was not good enough, you supplied your own drink. A German, Samuel Kiechel, described how, for safety's sake, he brought with him a hamper with nine large glass bottles. Three were unfortunately broken when his horse bolted and his sleigh tipped over.

French ambassador d'Avaux and his retinue travelled overland to Stockholm from Kalmar. (Kalmar Castle reflected in the water.)

Fences surrounded fields and meadows. (next pages)

Oysters were an important part of a 17th-century banquet. Royal couriers and oyster sellers were always first to be allotted fresh horses at inns along the highways.

Travelling by land was thus to be avoided, at any rate in summer. Winter travel was easier, since you could use a sleigh and make good speed across the ice.

In summer, boat was almost always the preferred means of travel. The downside was that a journey could take an indeterminate amount of time. Storms and dead calm were equally bad. A popular little handbook of medicinal advice for travellers recommended a proper travel dispensary of three casks of pills, balsam and 'teriak,' a universal cure whose most important ingredient was snake meat.

The French ambassador, d'Avaux and his entourage left Kalmar on Sunday 19 November 1634 to sail up to Stockholm. Three days later, they were back in Kalmar after three terrifying days on the Baltic. "I went to the barber to cut my hair, which was grey and on end from fear after those stormy days," wrote one of those onboard.

This magnificent sleigh belonged to Axel Oxenstierna. Sleighs were normally unadorned and without runners. They were like small boats. The traveller would be bedded down in the bottom, with a coachboy standing at the back.

The company decided to travel by land. A coach was out of the question. The cautious among them bought saddles and bridles; those who did not want to spend the money rode bareback.

As the ambassador's secretary Charles Ogier wrote, "The horses were small, but strong, spirited and unshod."

We can understand the burden for the peasants who had to lodge them along the route. The company had two hundred horses. A day's journey was usually fifty kilometres, or about thirty miles.

As usual when he was on dry land, Ogier was in excellent spirits. He described with humour how stablehands and serving girls would trot alongside the party, waiting to take the horses back home with them after the change.

Ogier thought the vicarages they visited looked like pigsties from the outside but found them less unpleasant inside. He wrote that there were even colourful paintings on the walls: "colourful and pretty, even if not done by Flemish or Italian masters."

They did not exchange saddles for coaches until they reached the city limits of Stockholm. They were splendid French coaches but almost unusable even in the capital. "Stockholm's position and the uneven roads do not really allow use of such magnificent vehicles," commented the Frenchman.

Later that year, Ogier tried transport by sleigh. It looked, according to the Frenchman, much like a coffin, but more comfortable. The passenger lay on the bottom, wrapped in bear and wolf skins. A Finnish coachboy stood at the back. The destination was Falun, some three hundred kilometres from Stockholm, and the trip was adventurous. The coachboy got lost, the sleigh tipped over and the Frenchman had to lodge in the most miserable hovels.

They could at least get up speed over snow and ice. King Karl XI set an unbeatable record half a century later: Stockholm to Kungsör on the west coast – a distance of 130 kilometres or 80 miles – in six and three quarter hours.

The first regular Swedish post-coach run was inaugurated in 1620, between Stockholm and Hamburg. There the yellow-clad mail-coach drivers of the German family-owned company, Thurn und Taxi, took over and delivered letters to Leiden University, and to Paris, Amsterdam and other important European cities.

The town wall of Visby on the island of Gotland. The island long enjoyed relative autonomy, interspersed with periods of Swedish or Danish rule. At the Peace of Brömsebro in 1645, Gotland formally became Swedish territory.

A postal service was a prerequisite to keep Sweden cohesive as it grew into a major power. The first real postal system dates from 1636. The plan proposed that farmhands working for the postal system be stationed every 20 kilometres or twelve and a half miles along the five most important arteries. These were the road from Stockholm due south to the Continent and the roads to Gothenburg, to the copper mining centre at Kopparberg, to the North and to Finland via the Åland archipelago.

What happened to those who robbed a royal courier was described in a court document from Stockholm, dated 2 November 1629. A courier, Cornelius Pederson, was on his way from Kalmar to Stockholm with letters from Chancellor Axel Oxenstierna to the King. The letters were the cease-fire agreement between Sweden and Poland and were stored in a special basket. There was also some money.

An early 17th-century trunk. It is leather-lined, with exotic decorations. Rich nobles travelled with large retinues and much luggage. Some nobles, however, were so poor that they were excused from their duties of travelling to the Riksdag or parliament in Stockholm.

In Kalmar, the royal courier joined up with a Filip Mats Eriksson. He was an ex-soldier and had been a prisoner of war in Poland. Cornelius Pederson decided to travel with Eriksson mostly because he felt sorry for him. He need not have. At a village just south of Söderköping, Filip Mats seized the basket, broke it open, and ran into the forest with the contents. He should not have. Catching the thief took only two days. The sentence was hanging and the King decreed it be carried out immediately. The executioner did the rest on 7 November.

Royal couriers had top priority but so did oyster transports. The reason was the extreme sensitivity of this delicacy, which was *de rigueur* on the banquet table of a 17th-century noble. Oysters were eaten *au naturel* but preferably prepared in some way. One example was the habit of stuffing chickens or capons with oysters and fresh butter. The bird was stitched up and more oysters were stuffed between the flesh and the skin. The delicacy was grilled on a skewer, basted with butter.

Gustavus Adolphus loved oysters. One problem was that the oyster banks of Bohuslän province belonged to Norway. This meant that oyster poaching became a profitable occupation for peasants in the region. The King's personal oyster poacher lived in the village of Ryr-Sundal in Dalsland province. "As long as he brings oysters from Norway," wrote the King, he was to be rewarded with six barrels of grain a year.

The Old Captain

ARCHAEOLOGISTS FOUND THE skeletal remains of 25 individuals on board the Vasa. Osteologist Ebba During measured them, fitted them together and analysed bone samples and was able to determine age, sex, height, injuries, illnesses and much more.

We shall resurrect one of them, a scarred, middle-aged man. He is known as Kalle, from the alphabetical list of names the osteologists made up for the skeletons. He was between 55 and 65 years old, 168 centimetres tall and had broken his leg at some stage earlier in his life. Kalle was found on the Vasa's upper gun deck. His remains were found lying on the starboard side and since the Vasa keeled over to the port side, he must have struggled up to windward and hung on, but not been able to escape. Being old, he might not have had the strength. But who was Kalle?

Captain Hans Jonsson drowned when the Vasa sank. This is probably his skull. Captain Jonsson discovered the major navigation channel through the islands to Stockholm harbour, still used today by large ships.

The Vasa sank in 1628 and sources tell us that one of the drowned was "old Captain Hans Jonsson." Much indicates that Hans Jonsson and the osteologists' Kalle are one and the same person. Hans Jonsson was born in the Stockholm archipelago. We know nothing of his early years but in the first decade of the 17th century, he was the commander of a number of battleships: the Lärkan, the Hollands Falken, the Jupiter, the Tre Kronor and the Leoparden.

Sometime in the early 1610s, Jonsson and his father made a discovery that was

Simple rocker beacons were used in Sweden in the early 17th century. The first real beacon was not built until 1651, at Landsort, the southern entrance to Stockholm.

to prove greatly beneficial for shipping and which brought him fame in contemporary naval circles. Close to the island where he was born, he found a deep channel that is still used today by all ships travelling to and from Stockholm by the southern route.

Hans Johnson's discovery means that large ships no longer had to struggle through the winding route known as "Seaman's Woe." Seamen would often have to drag, kedge (that is, haul with small anchors) or tow heavy ships. In reward, Hans Jonsson was given a property called Östra Ekedal "for lifelong tenancy, though the interest will be deducted from his wage." This was in 1616. He was also granted lifelong freedom from all payments for his home at Sollenkroka as well as the services of a farmhand. The King's condition was that Hans Jonsson would pilot naval warships through the new channel. This is certainly why he was onboard the Vasa on the unlucky afternoon of 10 August 1628.

The fleet used to assemble at Älvsnabben, an island in the south part of the Stockholm archipelago. It was the starting point for several of Gustavus Adolphus's military campaigns. Left on the island today is a wall surrounding a cemetery. Far more seamen fell victim to deficiency diseases and epidemics than died in battle.

Pilots have plied their trade in the Stockholm archipelago throughout the ages. Navigating the archipelago with all its reefs and islands was far more difficult than sailing by compass on the open sea or following a coastline. It was in fact out of the question to find a route through the thousands of islands without help. Any captain trying this would inevitably get lost or run aground. In the 1620s, the navy had thirty or so pilots.

"There is little use for a compass in this sea so filled of underwater skerries," wrote a despairing foreigner after a first encounter with the archipelago. This is quite true, especially since no reliable charts for the archipelago waters existed until the end of the 19th century. For this reason, pilots were often natives of the archipelago with sound local knowledge and there was little need for navigation marks. Posts, cairns, wooden crosses and other navigation marks were erected primarily in places where ships approached the coast and the archipelago's channels from the open sea. There were no lighthouses at the time. Sweden's first was lit in 1651 on Öja island in the southern part of the Stockholm archipelago. There had been pilots in the area for a hundred years. There were pilots on other islands as well including, from 1628, Älvsnabben, where the Vasa was headed For a long time, there was a collection box placed near the cottage with an admonitory verse:

The Stockholm archipelago has thirty thousand islands and skerries. It is impossible to navigate without a sea chart or local knowledge. (next pages)

Thou who have left the storms of sea
To find this peaceful strand
Where rays of hope content thee
Think of God and fatherland.

K
K
K
K
B
D
A
H

The Dance of Death

ADMIRAL HENRIK FLEMING's order to the fleet in 1628 was brutally realistic and ruthlessly demanding: "If it were to be, God forbid, that a ship be attacked so heavily by an enemy ship that all prominent officers are shot dead and there is no rescue, it would be desirable for an upstanding, loyal Swedish man to throw a brand into the gunpowder store."

Thus, if a Swedish ship is close to being captured by the enemy, some "upstanding Swedish" man should blow himself, the crew and the ship to kingdom come.

To transform a tired, sick and scared crew member into a brave, dedicated and strong fighting man demanded threats, punishment and beer. There was to be 250 litres of extra strong beer on every ship, to be shared out before battle to improve courage. The punishments decreed by maritime law were cruel and daunting. A brawler had his hand pinned to the main mast by a knife "so it was slit to the fingers." Anyone who caused a fire was himself thrown in the fire. A murderer was tied back-to-back with his victim and both were thrown overboard. Anyone who blasphemed or was insubordinate to the admiral or his officers was keelhauled.

"By a thousand devils and for God's sake, give me more wind!" shouted Admiral Nils Stiernsköld. In November 1627 Stiernsköld met a Polish fleet off Danzig. The Swedes suffered ignominious defeat, largely because of the limited experience of its commanding admiral.

Keelhauling was a common punishment, often tantamount to a death sentence. The provost marshal winched up the convicted man to a yardarm then dropped him headfirst into the water and he was pulled by a rope under the keel to the other side of the ship. Keelhauling was done "once, twice or three times, according to the nature of the offence." If the man did not drown, he ran a great risk of being ripped to pieces by the barnacles under the ship.

Surviving documents show that many were condemned to death for what are in our eyes modest crimes. But just how often the provost marshal actually carried out the execution is uncertain; often a sentence of death was commuted to corporal punishment such as being lashed or made to run the gauntlet.

According to Admiral Fleming's orders, it was important in battle to throw dead bodies down into the hold immediately. They would otherwise be in the way and ship's boys and young soldiers could be "timid and faint-hearted." And in battle, faint-hearted soldiers were of little use.

Battles both on dry land and on sea almost always terminated in hand-to-hand combat.

This was because 17th-century firearms – cannon, muskets and pistols – were heavy and unreliable and had disgracefully low rates of fire. In addition, accuracy was miserably bad and effective range extremely limited. A pistol was effective under ten metres. A musket ball would certainly kill a person at a couple of hun-

Muskets were heavy and cumbersome and had a dreadfully low rate of fire. It took several minutes to load a musket and when the musketeer was ready to fire, he had to rest his weapon on a special musket fork. The musket pictured was made in Stockholm in 1626, probably for navy use.

dred metres, but it was hardly possible to aim at and hit anything smaller than ships and big buildings at that range.

In fact, the crossbows and bows and arrows of the Middle Ages were far more effective weapons than 17th-century pistols and muskets, and easier to handle besides. A musket weighed ten kilos and to be able to even load and shoot, a musketeer had to rest his weapon on a special fork. Loading took several minutes and involved, besides, a balancing act that could cost a musketeer his life. A leather strap over the musketeer's left shoulder held black gunpowder in small leather cases; his left hand held a burning fuse and his heavy weapon. "Take care," wrote Admiral Fleming in his 1628 orders, "that the musketeers do not stand so close to each other that they set fire to each other's bandoleers." The bandoleer was the leather belt with gunpowder pouches. There was a great risk that the men would blow each other up.

The cannon were hard to handle as well. They were large, heavy pieces made of bronze and with low rate of fire. It took up to ten minutes to load and fire a cannon and demanded 66 different orders and actions:

A pewter flask discovered with the Vasa was found to contain alcohol, presumably rum. It was customary to give the crew a shot of spirits or a drink of beer before battle. It gave the faint-hearted more courage.

Remove plug ... Cover touchholes ... Take rammer ... Powderhorn up ... Open with your teeth ... Fuse ready ... Blow her out ... Fire!

King Gustavus Adolphus realised the limitations of his firearms and planned accordingly. He is justly famous as a moderniser of the art of war. He tried to develop weapons that were lighter and easier to handle; he also discarded the old Spanish battle tactics used in wars since the Middle Ages. This involved grouping foot soldiers in large, slow, compact rectangles, with musketeers and pike soldiers in rows, thirty men deep. This was a 'tercio,' and inside it most of the soldiers were immobilised in the middle, unable to shoot their muskets, hack with their swords or stab with their pikes. A tercio was a glacier, slowly grinding and crushing everything that came in its way with sheer volume and weight.

Gustavus Adolphus countered this with a hurricane of fire and movement. He formed his soldiers into lines, with three or six men in each. This let all musketeers shoot at the same time, and when they had fired, the pike soldiers leapt into the attack with lowered pikes. On the flanks, the King placed light cavalry, which attacked sword in hand. The opposing, continental cavalry fought, weighed down by heavy armour and at walking pace or a trot. Gustavus Adolphus's new tactics led to a great victory at Breitenfeldt in Saxony in 1631 and to Sweden's successes in the Thirty Years' War.

But fire and movement were also vital for battles fought at sea. There is an unpredictable factor in fighting at sea that no one can influence or change: the

wind. As long as large sailing ships were involved in battles at sea, the direction of the wind meant far more than the number of ships, men or cannon.

The fleet that lies to windward with its enemy to lee has all the advantages. It can attack at will and does not have to fear an enemy attack. It can flee if it believes the enemy to be stronger but does not have to worry about being caught.

The windward position was best because large ships beat against the wind badly and turn slowly through the wind. Tacking up to the enemy was slow and sometimes impossible.

A snap-lock pistol and spurs belonging to Chancellor-of-the-Realm Axel Oxenstierna. The pistol is a Scottish type, made in 1613. The spurs are of gilded steel.

The fickleness of the wind together with the clumsiness of large ships made it impossible to plan a battle the way it was done on land. Generals planned their battles according to the topography: hills, fields, forests and lakes. They built their fortifications on hills and placed their cannon with maximum elevation. Admirals, too, planned sea battles according to the topography: coastlines, islands, shallows

and deep channels. But they could not plan for the wind. And in northern climes, it can change from one day to the next, even from one hour to the next. A promising windward position can become a dangerous lee. It is as if the general's strategic hillock becomes a deep valley. A battle at sea was a dance of death where the deciding factors were seamanship, sophistication in warfare and plain luck. Commanding a fleet in battle may have been the most complicated task there was for a person living in the 17th century.

This is illustrated with frightening clarity by a sea battle which was fought between Swedish and Polish ships in November 1627. The battle took place off the Polish coast in the Gulf of Danzig. A Swedish fleet had been commanded to seal off the Polish ports, with the aim of stopping the Polish fleet from taking to sea.

The Swedish admiral was Nils Stiernsköld. He was 44 years old and had served in 1600 as page to Gustavus Adolphus's father, Duke Karl. By 1609 he was a field marshal in the war against Russia and from 1617 he was a councillor of the realm. Later, Stiernsköld held a number of high posts, among them, governor-general of Älvsborg, Dorpat and Baltiysk; and colonel of the fighting men of three Swedish provinces, Småland, Västergötland and Dalsland.

"Both the multi-faceted capability he showed and his engaging manner placed him high in the monarch's regard," wrote Nils Ahnlund, an authority on Gustavus Adolphus. He also noted that the King and Stiernsköld were similar in appearance, so much so that during Stiernsköld's tenure as governor-general of Älvsborg, he had an affair with a young woman who mistook him for the King.

On 1 November 1627 Nils Stiernsköld strode on board his flagship, the Tigern. He had lengthy experience of battles on land but none at all of sea warfare. In fact, he had commanded a ship only once, during a few uneventful summer days four years earlier when the fleet was mostly at anchor near Vaxholm in Stockholm's inner archipelago.

But this was the real thing. In the admiral's cabin on the Tigern, Stiernsköld made his battle plans. He would sail off to lure the Poles out to sea, but anchor out of sight behind a point. The next day, he would sail back and surprise the smaller, weaker Polish ships. It was a battle plan worthy of a general – but not an admiral. On 15 November, he put his plan into action. The Swedish fleet set sail on a course to the island of Öland, off the south-east Swedish coast, but dropped anchor behind the Hela peninsula, out of sight of the Poles. When Stiernsköld sailed back the next day, the Poles had fallen for the ruse and had sailed out into the Gulf of Danzig.

As Stiernsköld returned, the fresh north-easterly wind dropped and picked up

from the south. Stiernsköld, on the Tigern, tried to tack up to the Polish ships but failed. Horrified Swedish officers later described the admiral in desperation, swinging his sword above his head and calling on both God and the Devil: "By a thousand devils and for God's sake, give me more wind!" he shrieked from his command post in the stern. But by nightfall, he had not reached even one Polish ship that had run aground. The Tigern was forced to drop anchor, well isolated from the rest of the Swedish fleet.

When light came, the wind was still from the south and the Polish admiral, Dickmann, was quick to exploit the situation. He attacked the unprotected Stiernsköld and swiftly boarded and seized the Swedish flagship. Another of the bigger Swedish ships, the Solen, almost met the same fate, but was blown to bits by an 'upstanding' Swede rather than fall into Polish hands.

The battle lasted for only two hours but was a complete Polish victory, despite their smaller ships and fewer cannon. A Polish chronicler summed up the Battle of the Gulf of Danzig on 18 November 1627: "Listen, gentle reader. How pleasant it is to be able to chronicle the events outside Danzig, when the Solen (the sun) went down at midday, when it normally sets at night."

Admiral Nils Stiernköld is buried in Gillberga cemetery in the province of Södermanland, due south of Stockholm.

There was a variety of ammunition for the Vasa's cannon: pike-weights, chain-weights and pole-weights, which spun in the air when fired.

Entering Baltiysk harbour in Prussia, an important Swedish base in the 1620s. A watercolour from between 1627 and 1629 shows for the first time the three-tailed, blue and yellow Swedish naval ensign. *(next pages)*

Kirch
klein pillau
groß pill
Schanz
Tieff

An eyewitness account of the battle followed. It gives a realistic picture of the bloody inferno onboard a ship in battle: "The esteemed lord, Admiral Nils Stiernsköld, sailed slowly with his six ships in towards the stockade. When it was light, they spied their enemy's ships, both large and small, ten of them at the ready, all well-equipped with men and arms.

"When the ships met, the sea was calm. The enemy had a following breeze but our ships lay to the leeward. The enemy admiral attacked ours, and they shot at each other with cannon as long as they were at a distance from each other, but enemy hastened to board.

"Before this, the Esteemed Lord was shot by musket fire first in the throat and then a second time in the back. Captain Simon Siffvert was shot in the throat so that he tumbled into the hold. Many others, both of the enemy and of us, were shot down. Thereupon, the enemy admiral brought up two more ships alongside Master Nils Stiernsköld. They were the Ritter S:t Georg on the right side and the Denen on the left; then came a third ship behind and fired at the Esteemed Lord's ship. When he went to leave his cabin, a ball came and hit him on his left arm so that he fell over. He wished to raise himself on several occasions but the power within him was weak.

"Meanwhile, the Esteemed Lord's servant, Mats by name, was shot in both arms so that his flesh hung loose. When there was no more to be done, the bugler sounded quarters, upon which the enemy boarded the ship and cut down some of our men. The enemy admiral was thereupon shot so that he fell dead.

"With now his wailing enemy running rampage on his ship, the Esteemed Lord lay in his cabin, with his servant Mats on a chair, saying: 'Here I sit and there lies my lord.' Then the Esteemed Lord asked for both priest and surgeon. The servant Mats partook of the sacraments and one of his enemy's barbers cut him on both arms and he gave up his spirit. The Esteemed Lord let his enemy barber cut him on the arm as well and called upon the priest, whose name was Bartholdus. When he felt his time was nigh, he took the priest's hand in his own bloody one and said: 'Dear Mister Bartholdus, tell me no other thing than that the Lord Jesus will receive my soul.' Thereupon he fell sweetly asleep in his Maker, having lived 44 years, 27 weeks and five days."

The Poles brought the Tigern back to Danzig. and not before chancellor Axel Oxenstierna had negotiated with them could Stiernsköld's body be returned. It arrived back in Stockholm on a ship decorated with flags and black cloth in July 1628. The Vasa was moored at the same quay, waiting for its maiden voyage a couple of weeks later. From the Vasa's cannon came a salute for a fallen hero.

THE JOURNEY OF THE VASA

1. SKEPPSGÅRDEN SHIPYARD
The Vasa was built here.

2. THREE CROWNS CASTLE
Where cannon and ballast were loaded, and where the fateful voyage began on 10 August 1628.

3. TRANBODARNA
The Vasa set its sails.

4. THE SHIPWRECK SITE
The Vasa keeled over and sank after a journey of little more than 1,000 metres. In 1956, Anders Franzén found the ship.

5. BECKHOLMEN ISLAND
After salvage in 1961, the Vasa was towed to a dry dock on the island. This is where the early archaeological work was done.

6. ALKÄRRET
The ship was kept in continuous conservation in a provisional museum on this site between 1961 and 1988.

7. GALÄRVARVET SHIPYARD
The Vasa was towed here on a pontoon in December 1988. In June 1990, the price-winning, custom-designed Vasa Museum was inaugurated.

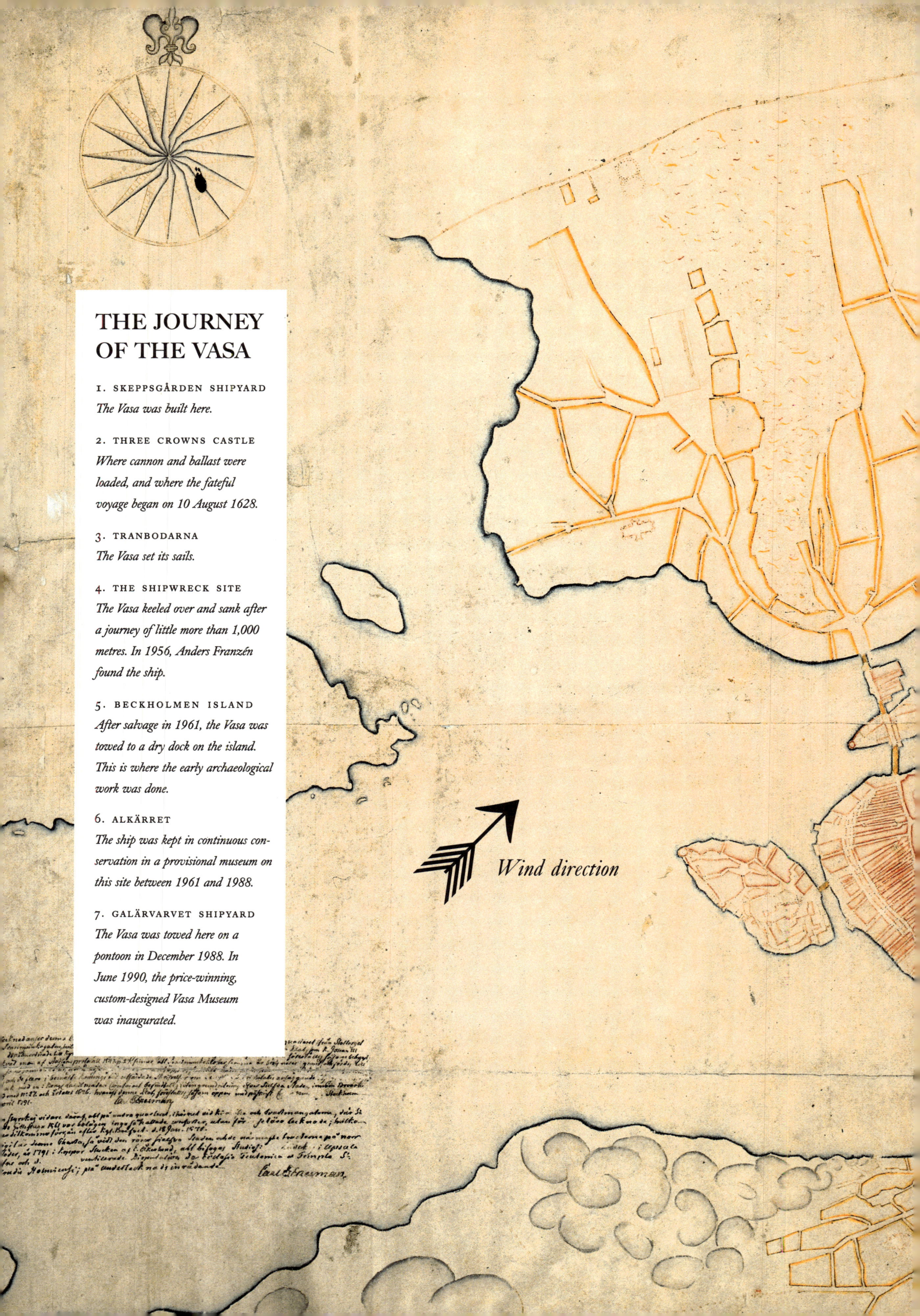

This is the oldest preserved map of Stockholm, dating from the 1620s.

p 5 Map of Stockholm from about 1640. Royal Library, Stockholm.

A time of lions

p 10 Saxon cavalry standard. Royal Army Museum, Stockholm.
p 12 Gunport. Vasa Museum.
p 14 Lion timepiece. Skokloster.
p 15 Sculpture on the Vasa's bow. Painted replica. Vasa Museum.
p 16 The Vasa's stern. Vasa Museum.
p 17 The Vasa's lion figurehead. Vasa Museum.
p 18 Queen Maria Eleonora's pewter coffin. Design by Henrik De la Vallée and made in 1659. Riddarholm church, Stockholm.
p 19 Preserved lion from 1732. Gripsholm palace.
p 21 Coat of arms of the noble Lejonankar family. House of the Nobility, Stockholm.
p 22 King Gustavus II Adolphus. Oil painting by David Klöcker Ehrenstrahl and sculpture from the Vasa. Replicas. Vasa Museum.
p 24 Sculpture on the Vasa's bow. Replica. Vasa Museum.
p 26 Beacon at Möja, Stockholm archipelago.
p 28 Wax portrait of King Gustavus II Adolphus, from the Augsburg chest of wonders of 1632. Uppsala University.
p 29 Board game counter bearing portrait of King Sigismund. Lars Broberg, Stockholm.
p 30 King Gustavus II Adolphus lands in Germany. Artist: Johan Hammer. 1670s. Karlbergs castle, Stockholm.
p 31 Gloves and spectacles, from the Augsburg chest of wonders of 1632.Uppsala University.
p 33 Småland.
p 35 Miniature of Ebba Brahe in ivory casket. Skokloster.
p 36 Gustav Gustavsson of Vasaborg. Coat of arms, House of the Nobility, Stockholm.
p 37 Ebba Brahe's garden pavilion, Bockhammar, Västmanland.
p 38 South-facing window, Kalmar castle.
p 39 Queen Maria Eleonora's regal diadem. Royal Palace, Stockholm.
p 40 Princess Kristina's pewter coffin. Riddarholm church, Stockholm.
p 41 Queen Kristina. Oil painting by Jacob Heinrich Elbfas, 1634. Gripsholm palace.
p 42 Mooring ring on Kapell Island, Älvsnabben, Stockholm's archipelago.
p 44 King Gustavus Adolphus's red morocco slippers. Royal Armoury, Stockholm.
p 45 Princess Kristina's letter to King Gustavus Adolphus, 1632. National Archives of Sweden, Stockholm.
p 46 Queen Maria Eleonora. Nationalmuseum, Stockholm. Photo: Nationalmuseum.
p 47 Linen cloth, 1632. Royal Armoury, Stockholm.
p 48 Aged Hercules. Sculpture on the Vasa by Mårten Redtmer. Vasa Museum.
p 49 Roof of the House of Nobility, Stockholm.
p 50 King Gustavus Adolphus's Berik-armour. Royal Armoury, Stockholm.
p 52 Ornamentation on organ of Bälinge church, Uppland. Sculptor: Mårten Redtmer.
p 53 Ornamentation on organ of Övertorneå church, Norrbotten. Sculptor: Mårten Redtmer. Replica. Vasa Museum.
p 54 Ornamentation on organ of Bälinge Church, Uppland. Sculptor: Mårten Redtmer.
p 56 Coat of arms of the Vasa dynasty, on the Vasa's stern. Vasa Museum.
p 57 A wood carver's tools. 17th century. Skokloster.
p 58 Hercules. 16th-century ceiling painting. Kalmar castle.
p 60 Sculpture on the Vasa. Painted replica. Vasa Museum.
p 61 Hercules. 17th-century bronze sculpture. Drottningholm castle park, Stockholm.

Insight and perspective

p 64 Engraved ostrich egg. 17th century. Skokloster.
p 65 The Church of St. Peter in Rome.
p 66 Inkwell and quill, from the Augsburg chest of wonders of 1632. Uppsala University.
p 67 Collected works of Shakespeare, 1632. Royal Library, Stockholm.
p 68 Virgin forest. Tyresta National Park, Södermanland.
p 71 Souvenir from Bethlehem. 17th century. Skokloster.
p 73 Rembrandt. Self-portrait, 1628. Rijksmuseum, Amsterdam.
p 74 Canal Grande and the Santa Maria della Salute Church, Venice.
p 75 Carved nautilus shell. 17th century. Skokloster.
p 76 17th-century ship. Church tower at Hoorn.
p 77 Onion domes, Kremlin, Moscow.
p 79 Garden, Katsura Imperial Palace, Kyoto.

Where ships almost brush the houses

p 80 Entering Stockholm harbour. W.I. Blaeuw, Seespiegel, 1627. Royal Military Archives, Stockholm.
p 82 Cabbage in the garden of the Vasa Museum. 17th-century vegetables, spices and medicinal plants are grown here.
p 84 Stockholm. Pencil drawing. Early 17th century. Royal Library, Stockholm. Photo: Royal Library.
p 86 Axel Oxenstierna's palace, 1653. Stockholm.
p 88 Paintings by Roland Johansson Öberg, 1699. Barsta Chapel, Ångermanland. The chapel was built in 1655.
p 89 The fortlet at Dalarö, Södermanland.
p 90 Riddarholm church, Stockholm.
p 92 Fire-fighting equipment. 17th century. Skokloster.
p 93 Inn. Pencil drawing. From Magalotti, *Sweden in 1674*. Royal Library, Stockholm.
p 96 Bone drinking horn. Early 17th century. Lars Broberg, Stockholm.
p 97 The Prodigal Son. Embroidery, signed 1635. Museum of the City of Göteborg. Photo: Museum of the City of Göteborg.
p 98 Lead-glazed ceramic bowls. Vasa Museum.
p 99 Casked beer tankards. Vasa Museum.
p 100 Inn in the province of Skåne. Oil painting by Govert Camphuysen. Malmö Museum, Malmö. Photo: Malmö Museum.
p 102 Women emptying latrine barrels. From Magalotti, *Sweden in 1674*. Royal Library, Stockholm.
p 105 Combination lock on chest. Vasa Museum.
p 106 Skeleton Beata. Vasa Museum.
p 107 Copper Matt. Bronze replica. Artist: Mårten Redtmer. Vasa Museum.
p 108 Dice, bone cup, backgammon board with picture of King Gustavus Adolphus, purse, board game. Lars Broberg, Stockholm.
p 109 Italian lute. Made by Vendelio Venere. Early 17th century. Music Museum, Stockholm.
p 110 Angel playing the lute. Ornamentation on organ of Bälinge church, Uppland. Sculptor: Mårten Redtmer.
p 111 16th-century ivory cornett. Boxwood shawm from about 1680.Music Museum, Stockholm.
p 112 Clay pipes. Vasa Museum.
p 113 Backgammon game. Vasa Museum.
p 114 Split cod, Iceland.
p 116 Inn interior, 17th century. Oil painting by David Teniers. Vasa Museum Archive.

The Saga of the Vasa

p 118 The Vasa's port side.
p 122 Brita Bååt to Ängsö. Unsigned oil painting from 1620s. Ängsö manor, Uppland.
p 123 Ängsö manor, Uppland.
p 124 Arndt De Groot's signature. The main naval shipyard documents. National Archives of Sweden, Stockholm.
p 126 17th-century compasses. Private owner.
p 127 The main naval shipyard, Stockholm, 1634. Detail from portrait of Queen Kristina, by Jacob Heinrich Elbfas. Gripsholm palace.
p 128 Gunports on the Vasa.
p 129 The Kronobageri (the royal bakery), Stockholm.
p 130 Gulf of Riga.
p 132 King Gustavus II Adolphus's signature. National Archives of Sweden, Stockholm.
p 133 Coat of arms of the noble Ekstubbe family. House of Nobility, Stockholm.
p 134 Calendarium Perpetuum. Early 17th century. Lars Broberg, Stockholm.
p 137 Helmsman's post on the Vasa.
p 138 The Vasa's upper deck.
p 140 Abraham Brahe's diary. National Archives of Sweden, Stockholm.
p 141 The Vasa's anchor cable. Vasa Museum.
p 142 Model of the Vasa, scale 1:10, by Göran Forss. Vasa Museum.
p 144 Model of the palace Tre Kronor (Three Crowns). Stockholm City Museum.
p 146 17th-century diving bell. Copy in Vasa Museum.
p 147 Barrel for providing air to diver. Illustration from Mårten Triewald, *The Art of Living under the Waters*, 1743. Royal Library, Stockholm
p 149 24-pounder bronze cannon from the Vasa. Vasa Museum.
p 150 Tools for divers. Illustration from Mårten Triewald, *The Art of Living under the Waters*, 1743. Royal Library, Stockholm.
p 151 Title page. Mårten Triewald, *The Art of Living under the Waters*, 1743. Royal Library, Stockholm.
p 152 The waters of Stockholm. It was here Anders Franzén plumbed the depths in 1956 and found the Vasa. Replica.
p 153 Anders Franzén and the core sampler he used in his quest for the Vasa.
p 154 Head diver Per Edvin Fälting and Anders Franzén during diving operations on the Vasa. Vasa Museum Archives.
p 156 Shipworm traces in the wood. Vasa Museum.
p 156 Salvaging and excavation of the Vasa, 1961. Photo: Vasa Museum Archives.
p 157 Skeleton found during excavation of Vasa. Photo: Vasa Museum Archives.
p 158 Diver by one of the Vasa's sculptures. Photo: Vasa Museum Archives.
p 160 The Vasa's bowsprit.
p 161 Wooden spoons, wooden bowl and pewter box. Vasa Museum.
p 162 The Vasa Museum from the northwest.
p 163 The Vasa figurehead and lower mast.

Running before the wind between the Pillars of Hercules

p 164 Anamorphoscope, from the Augsburg chest of wonders of 1632.Uppsala University.
p 166 Title page. Francis Bacon, *Instauratio magna*, London, 1665. Royal Library, Stockholm.
p 168 Tycho Brahe. Unsigned oil painting. 17th century. Skokloster.
p 169 Celestial globe, 1625, by Petrus Plancius, Amsterdam. Skokloster.
p 170 Augsburg chest of wonders of 1632. Uppsala University.
p 171 Noble coat of arms. House of Nobility, Stockholm.
p 173 Gustavianum, Uppsala.
p 174 Engraved powder-horn of bone. Early 17th century. Lars Broberg, Stockholm.
p 175 Axel Oxenstierna. Drawing in charcoal and coloured chalk by Daniel Dumonstier, 1634. Royal Swedish Academy of Letters, History and Antiquities.
p 176 Hunting scene, ceiling of Kalmar castle. 16th century.
p 178 Cutlery and pewter plate. British made. Early 17th century. Skokloster.
p 179 Sweden, 1626. Andreas Bureus.s map. Royal Library, Stockholm.
p 180 Flax drying, Hälsingland.
p 182 Forge at Vira Bruk, Uppland.
p 183 Copper mine at Falun. Drawing by Hans Ranié, 1683. Detail.
p 184 Silver mine at Sala, Västmanland.
p 185 Copper mine at Falun. Drawing by Hans Ranié, 1683. Detail.
p 186 Copper coin minted at Sala and Arboga in the 1620s. Found on the Vasa. Vasa Museum.
p 187 Copper mine at Falun, Dalarna.
p 188 Leaves of blue anemone (hepatica nobilis).
p 189 Mandrake root.
p 190 Leeching glass and bloodletting tools, from the Augsburg chest of wonders of 1632. Uppsala University.

Thanks

During the nearly ten years we spent planning, photographing and making an inventory for this book, we were given invaluable help by a large number of amiable and skilful people. First and foremost, we would like to extend thanks to our friends at the Vasa Museum: Klas Helmerson, Hans Soop, Katarina Schoerner, Urban Skenbäck and Katarina Villner. You read, commented on, corrected and augmented. Ebba During at Sweden's Osteological Institution gave life to those who died on the ship. Antique dealer Lars Broberg was extremely helpful with his wide knowledge of 17th-century objects. We would also like to thank the staff at Gripsholm Castle, the Royal Collections, the National War Archives, the Royal Library, the Royal Armoury, the Music Museum, the National Archives of Sweden, Skokloster Castle and the Museum Gustavianum Uppsala University Museum. And finally, thanks to Catharina Piper, the Lady of Ängsö Manor, where once oaks were felled to build the ship and the saga began.

Erling Matz *Hans Hammarskiöld*

The pictures in the book were taken between 1997 and 1999. All pictures of objects and all still lifes were taken with cameras and lenses by Hasselblad. Nikon equipment was used for the other pictures. Fuji film was used throughout, principally Superia. The Vasa Museum is on Djurgården island in Stockholm. For information and opening times, call +46 8 519 548 00 or go to www.vasamuseum.se or www.vasamuseum.com. Glorious Vasa is also available in Swedish, I lejonets tid (ISBN 91-89204-16-6), and German, Die Vasa (ISBN 91-89204-18-2).

Glorious Vasa was printed on environmentally friendly, Nordic Swan labelled Munken Lynx 150 gsm. paper, manufactured by Munkedals AB, SE-455 81 Munkedal, Sweden. Tel: +46 524 17 000, fax: +46 524 12 533, market@munkedals.se, www.munkedals.se.